TO

FROM

DATE

A LYRICAL DEVOTIONAL

belovedness

OVERCOMING YOUR INNER CRITIC

sarah kroger

Belovedness: Overcoming Your Inner Critic: A Lyrical Devotional

First Edition, May 2025

Published by:

21154 Highway 16 East
Siloam Springs, AR 72761
dayspring.com

Written by: Sarah Kroger
Content Collaboration by: Margot Starbuck
Cover Design by: Hannah Brinson

Printed in China
Prime: U3369
ISBN: 979-8-88603-028-0

CONTENTS

WAKING UP TO BELOVEDNESS

LIVING AS THE BELOVED

INTRODUCTION

WAKING UP TO BELOVEDNESS

I was sitting in a room at the Integrity Music offices in Nashville with two other writers, working on some new songs. If you're not familiar with this process, writers usually gather in a room and simply have a conversation. Eventually the inspiration starts to flow, and you continue trading melody and lyric ideas until something sticks—and then you chase after it.

My co-writers, Michael and Tony, and I were in the middle of writing a different song. We had paused the process to share about how God had been moving in our lives lately.

"I've been on this journey of trying to own my belovedness," I said. I've been asking myself how my life would look different if I lived from that place of being totally and completely loved by God."

As I continued sharing about this journey that I'd been on, Michael interrupted and said, "We've got to write that song."

And within moments that first line, "You've owned your fear . . ." was filling the room.

"As you were talking, this line popped into my head," Michael explained. And he started playing what would become the first verse.

And then the line came that set the tone for the rest of the write: ". . . it's time to own your belovedness."

When Tony and I heard it, we just looked at each other wide-eyed.

I confirmed, "We have to write this right now."

With some songs, you have to wrestle them to the ground to get them out. But "Belovedness" was like a *download* from above. It practically fell into our laps . . . and I'm so thankful we were prepared to catch it.

My journey to "own" my belovedness had begun a few years earlier when I read a book called *Life of the Beloved* by a Catholic priest and spiritual writer named Henri Nouwen. As I read it, my eyes were opened to some game-changing truths. Like the ways I was tangled up in the comparison trap, or how I'd been letting my fears bully me. As I looked back over my life, I could see I'd been living this way for years. But from the moment I began to read Nouwen's words, the trajectory of my life with God began to change. I committed to intentionally embracing what is most true about me, and what is most true about you: our *belovedness*.

The ways that people have responded to this song have blown me away. While I knew it meant something special to *me*, I never could have imagined it would reach and impact others the way that it has.

> *I get messages about the song on social media. People come up to me at concerts with tears in their eyes, sharing stories of how it's touched them personally. A single woman told me, "I listen to that song every day on the way to work." A mom of young kids offered, "My daughters listen to that song as they're falling asleep at night. I'm so grateful they have this song to remind them of their belovedness when they're young." A priest shared, "Thank you so much. This song has been a massive part of my healing journey."*

Truly, the impact of this song has been greater than I ever could have anticipated. And while I was invited to steward it, it's worth remembering that stewards take care of something that doesn't belong to them. I'm so glad this song is out in the world. After all, it's not mine to hold. And I continue to be grateful for every person who has shared with me, along the way, about how a song that was born from my story has intersected with their own.

HERE'S HOW IT WORKS

Have you ever listened to a song and marveled at how relevant it was to your life? Our favorite songs speak directly to our hearts. Our souls. Our experiences.

The same thing is true about books. The best ones connect with our own experience. They meet a need we may not have even known we had. This book isn't about *me*; it's about *you*. My prayer is that it will be a vehicle for you to discover what these lyrics—and the rich meaning behind them—have to do with you. With your experience. With your belovedness.

In each of the entries, I've broken down the song into smaller bites, lyric by lyric. I share what it has meant to me and what it might mean for you.

I've also included a few questions for you to reflect on. I encourage you to spend time with these in whatever way works best for you. You can simply close your eyes and noodle on them for a bit. You can invite God to be your helper, and conversation partner, as you assume a prayerful posture of meditation. You can explore these ideas through journaling, making connections with your own life.

After the reflection questions, I've included a verse from God's Word for you to hold onto—memorize it so you can remind yourself of it when your inner critic gets loud. There's nothing more powerful than speaking Truth to silence the lies.

At the end of each day's reflection, I've offered a prayer for you to pray. You can read it quietly; you can speak it aloud; you can write it in your journal. You can even use it as a springboard for your own conversation with God.

This book has been designed for you to engage with God in a new way as He helps you to recognize and embrace your inherent and undeniable belovedness.

You've owned your fear and all
your self-loathing
You've owned the voices inside of
your head
You've owned the shame and
reproach of your failure
It's time to own your belovedness

You've owned your past and how
it's defined you
You've owned everything
everybody else says
It's time to hear what your Father
has spoken
It's time to own your belovedness

He says, "You're mine, I smiled
when I made you
I find you beautiful in every way
My love for you is fierce and
unending
I'll come to find you, whatever it
takes
My beloved"

You've owned the mess you see in
the mirror
You've owned the lies that you're
just not enough
You've been so blinded by all you're
comparing
It's time to own your belovedness

He says, "You're mine, I smiled
when I made you
I find you beautiful in every way
My love for you is fierce and
unending
I'll come to find you, whatever it
takes
My beloved"

You are completely loved and fully
known
Beloved, believe He died to make
your heart His home

And He says, "You're mine, I smiled
when I made you
I find you beautiful in every way
My love for you is fierce and
unending
I'll come to find you, whatever it
takes"

He says, "You're mine, I smiled
when I made you
I find you beautiful in every way
My love for you is fierce and
unending
I'll come to find you, whatever it
takes
My beloved"

It's time to own your belovedness

You've owned your fear . . .

Belovedness

SARAH KROGER

0:08 3:42

OWN WHAT IS MOST TRUE

About a decade ago, I could've convinced anyone that I was thriving. I was happily married, I was writing and performing my own music, I was leading worship—my dream job. But I knew I wasn't living in freedom. In every room I stepped into, I was afraid to stand out in any way. Every time I'd take the stage, I felt like I was hitting a wall. Instead of just taking inspiration from other artists, I was constantly comparing myself to them. And no matter how I "performed" or how people responded, in my mind, I'd always come up short. This often left me feeling like a fraud, or even worse, a failure. As God opened my eyes, I came to see that so much of my potential was being stunted by my fears.

Consider what fear does to us. If you spot a herd of buffalo stampeding toward you, your body is designed to explode with fear. That surge of adrenaline fuels you to run for your life. God created us with emotions *for our good*. Fear, sadness, anger, and joy are the body's way of communicating something we need to know. Fear, sadness, and anger are all natural responses to trauma and pain. But when the hurt is allowed to fester, when we don't face our pain, those same feelings can turn on us and begin to bully us. That's where I was. Rather than facing the messiness of my past, I tried to ignore it, and it turned on me.

In *Life of the Beloved*, Henri Nouwen writes, "Every time you feel hurt, offended, or rejected, you have to dare to say to yourself: 'These feelings, strong as they may be, are not telling me the truth about myself. Even though I cannot feel it right now, the truth is that I am the chosen child of God, precious in God's eyes, called the Beloved from all eternity, and held safe in an everlasting embrace.'"[1] Nouwen's holy words were an invitation, to me, to own my inherent belovedness. They set me on a path to discover my identity as a beloved child of God.

We're all trying to figure out who we are, right? I think too often we write the "good parts" about ourselves in pencil and the "bad parts" in pen—or in thick permanent marker. We look in the mirror, and we *own* all the ways we believe we're *not* good enough. We don't simply hear them and let them roll off our backs. Instead, we treat them as gospel truth.

The reality is that we are all pilgrims on a journey. We have not yet arrived; we are works in progress. We are sinners who will

---

1. Henri Nouwen, *Life of the Beloved: Spiritual Living in a Secular World* (New York: Crossroad Publishing, 1992), 59.

make some mistakes and take some hits. But we fear that these shortcomings define us. Rather, the *core* of our identity is that we are loved by God. Period.

Maybe, like me, you've been living in fear. One woman looks in the mirror and hates what she sees staring back at her. One man catches his reflection in a storefront window and worries that his bad choices will destroy him. A child living in a chaotic home tries to be good so that he or she won't be left alone. Sometimes we don't even notice that we're allowing our fears to drive us.

I'm still on the journey to embrace my belovedness. Every day I have to make the choice to believe the truth of who I am and to reflect the glory that God has put in my life. Nouwen's invitation to me all those years ago—to embrace the fullness of my belovedness—is the same one I want to extend to you. Romans 11:29 tells us, "For God's gifts and His call can never be withdrawn" (NLT). You were not made to be owned by your fears. Rather, the unalterable and undeniable truth is that you were created, from the beginning, as *beloved*. It's who you are. And nothing could ever take that away.

QUESTIONS TO ASK YOURSELF

Do I know, in the depths of my heart,

what it is to be beloved?

What are the lies, beliefs, or thoughts that are bullying me? What is owning me today?

Am I ready and willing to embark on this journey?

SCRIPTURE

SPEAK, LORD,

FOR YOUR SERVANT

IS LISTENING.

I SAMUEL 3:9

PRAYER

God, as You show me my heart, I can see how I've allowed fears to own me. Help me to find myself in You. Remind me that my feelings, and the thoughts that spring from them, do not define me. Only You can define me. And You say that I am Your beloved, chosen child. I am precious in Your sight. And from the beginning of time, I have been Yours. Lord, be with me on this journey. Teach me how to embrace my belovedness daily. Open the eyes of my heart, and open my ears to hear Your voice, that I might embrace the truth of who I am: Beloved.

AMEN.

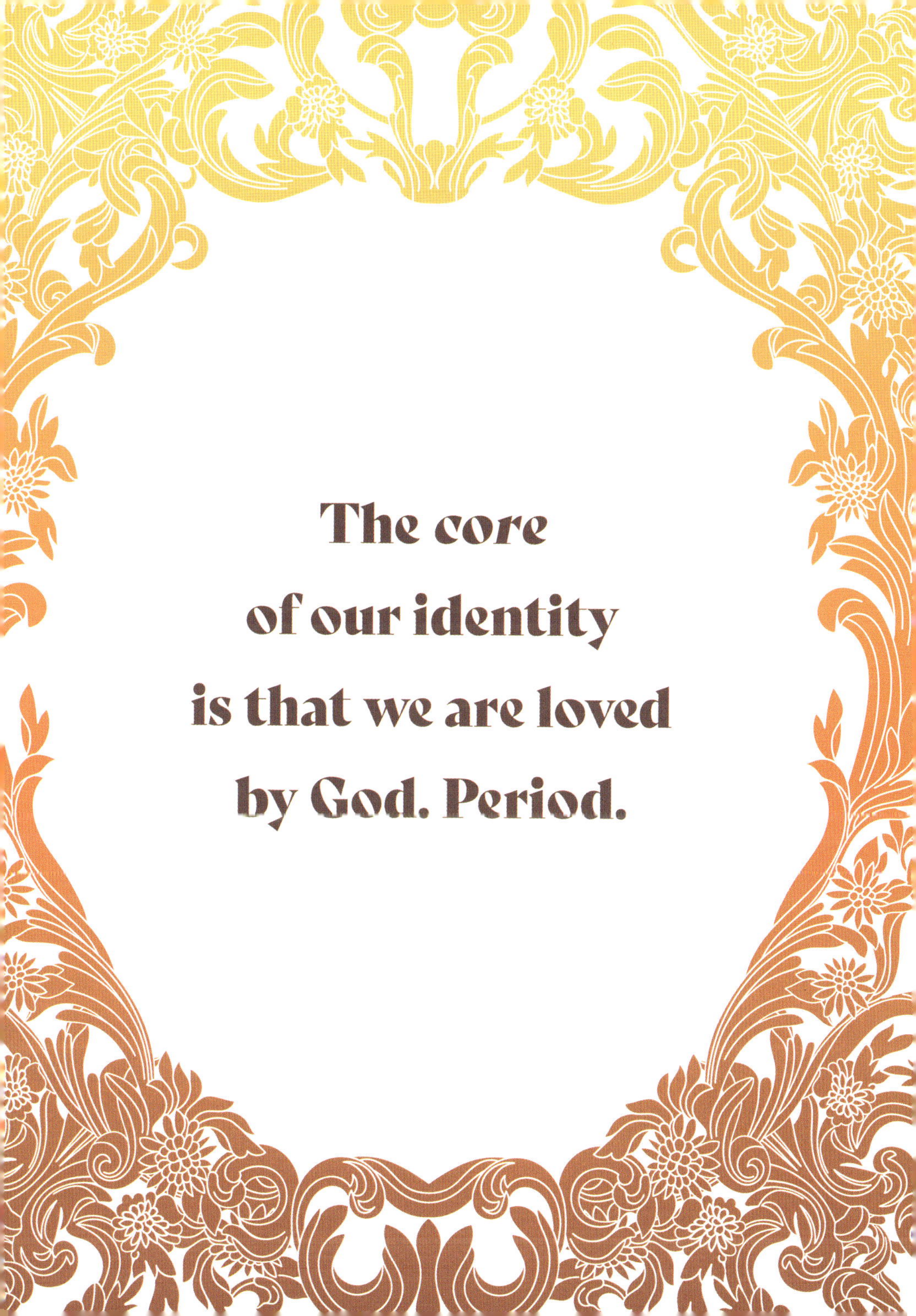
The core
of our identity
is that we are loved
by God. Period.

. . . all
your
self-
loathing . . .

Belovedness

SARAH KROGER

0:11 3:42

HURLING DOWN THE ACCUSER

What is your problem?!

I used to have this terrible habit of being unnecessarily self-critical. If I got stuck during a writing session, or if I felt like I messed up onstage or in an interview—or even in a conversation with a friend—I would start spiraling. The critic in my head would bully me, saying, *What is your problem? You're so bad at this.* It was a negative-self-talk tape loop that seemed to roll on repeat.

Henri Nouwen offers insight, explaining, "These negative voices are so loud and persistent that it is easy to believe them. That's the great trap. It is the trap of self-rejection."[2]

As if other people's opinions aren't enough to deal with, it's amazing how we can actually bully *ourselves*, hurling insult after insult.

I wonder what that voice sounds like in your head. What are the ways that it accuses you?

You're too this.

You're too that.

You're so stupid. You can't do it.

---

2. Nouwen, *Life of the Beloved*, 31.

No one likes you.

You'll never be enough.

That nasty, overly critical voice is not the voice of God. It is the voice of the enemy. And the enemy is interested in our downfall, not in our well-being. The book of Revelation identifies the devil as "the accuser." He points a finger at us and tries to make us feel ashamed. He tries only to bring trouble, not the truth. But we don't resign ourselves to defeat, because there is good news in the end. "The accuser of our brothers and sisters, who accuses them before our God day and night, has been hurled down" (Revelation 12:10).

Today, though? Today we are easily bullied by our negative thoughts. And it's likely because we're the only ones who can hear those inner voices. Our friends can't overhear them and correct them! We have to identify the voice, because we can't overcome anything that we don't expose to the light. Thankfully, we can learn how to recognize the voice of the accuser. I started using a filter, asking myself, *What would I do if a friend said that to me?* (Try it! It helps!) And more often than not, I'd think, *How dare you! Don't speak to me like that!* When you begin to recognize those voices, I encourage you to externalize them like that. How would you respond if someone else said that to you? And how would you respond if you heard those words spoken to someone you love?

If a friend said some of the things to us that we say to ourselves, they would no longer be our friend. And yet we allow our internal chatterbox to persist, often without even realizing it.

Slowly, I've begun to pull back the curtain on what had been hidden. I shared with those whom I trusted about the inner battle I'd been facing. Even though they couldn't fix it for me, I discovered by opening up that I wasn't the only one who was fighting against lies. In fact, I couldn't believe how common it was. I'm so grateful for the gift of community. There were so many people in that season who continued to love and support me by speaking truth over my life when I let them see the real me.

I also began to speak truth to myself whenever I would start spiraling in my head. I tried to approach myself with kindness rather than judgment. I would say to myself things like, *You are not your mistakes. Everyone messes up. You can try again tomorrow.*

You'll never be perfect, but that doesn't make you any less loved. The voice of truth is *kind.* And just like God helps you to uncover and reveal the enemy's lies, God's Spirit also helps you to hear and affirm what is most true.

Beloved, the enemy—the accuser—lies to you about who you are. But as you unmask him, you can choose to listen to what is most true.

QUESTIONS TO ASK YOURSELF

What negative self-talk scrolls through my mind?

Who is someone in my life who speaks to
me with consistent kindness?

Do I speak to myself with kindness?
And if I don't, how can I start to do so?

SCRIPTURE

THE ACCUSER OF
OUR BROTHERS AND SISTERS,
WHO ACCUSES THEM BEFORE
OUR GOD DAY AND NIGHT,
HAS BEEN HURLED DOWN.
THEY TRIUMPHED OVER HIM
BY THE BLOOD OF THE LAMB
AND BY THE WORD OF
THEIR TESTIMONY.

—REVELATION 12:10–11

PRAYER

Gracious Father, I'm leaning into the sound of Your voice today, listening for the words of truth You speak. Help me to hear what is kind, what is good, what is true. Lord, I offer my heart and mind to You. You hear it all, even the things I say to myself that no one else hears. Replace the lies of the enemy with the truth about who I am, who You are, and who others are. Continue to walk with me on this journey to embrace my belovedness.

AMEN.

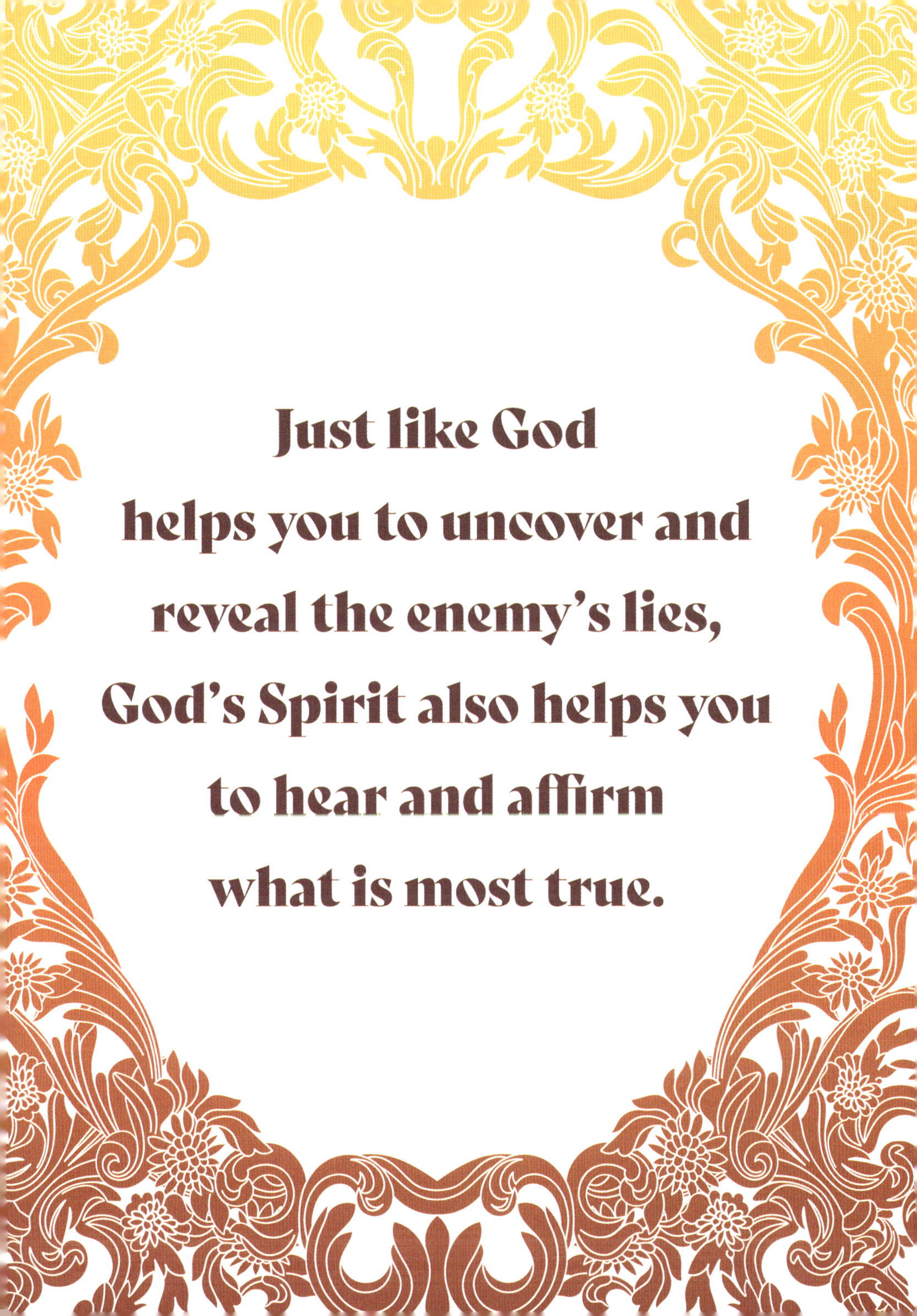
Just like God
helps you to uncover and
reveal the enemy's lies,
God's Spirit also helps you
to hear and affirm
what is most true.

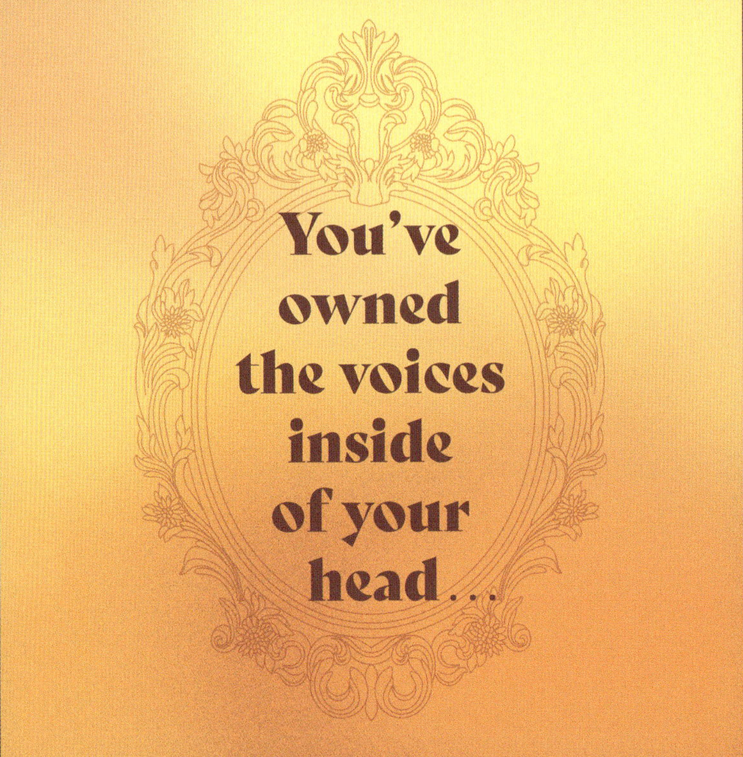

Belovedness

SARAH KROGER

0:13 3:42

THE VOICE THAT LIES

Are you the kind of person who wakes up with a smile, ready to face whatever the day brings with courage and joy? Or do you wake up feeling grumpy, ready to snap at anyone who looks at you the wrong way?

How we start our day makes all the difference.

One bright summer morning, I began my day in the way I usually do. Sitting in my kitchen, I was sipping some coffee, giving my brain time to slowly kick into gear. On this particular day, though, I had my phone in my hand. That was my first mistake. With every app I clicked on, a question echoed in my heart . . .

Opening my email app, I wondered, *Am I needed?*

Scrolling through my Instagram feed, I wondered, *Am I liked?*

Flipping through text messages, I wondered, *Is anyone thinking of me?*

I suspect I'm not alone. All of us can be tempted to slide into this rut. It's easy to get caught in the loop of wondering, to get sucked into the cycle of questioning our worth. When it becomes most dangerous is when we don't notice we're doing it! Because if we don't notice that questioning of our hearts, we allow the answers to come from our email in-box. Or our Instagram feed. Or our text messages.

Thankfully, on that morning, I was interrupted. After several minutes of mindlessly scrolling, I heard a Voice in my spirit say, *Why are you going to these places to find out who you are?*

Have you heard that Voice before?

It may ask: *Why are you looking to success—in school or at work—to gauge your worth? Why are you looking to dating relationships to find out who you are? Why are you looking at the bulges and blemishes you see in the mirror to determine your value?*

If you're anything like me, you know that those metrics aren't reliable, but like a roaring tide, they can still catch us up in their torrents before we know it. However, when I'm in my right mind, I *know* that the things of this world will never satisfy.

This internal wondering about our value isn't a new phenomenon. In fact, it reminds me of one of my favorite stories in all of Scripture: the account of the woman at the well (see John 4). Scholars have guessed that this Samaritan woman went to the well in the heat of the day just to avoid the stares and gossip of those in her community who whispered lies about her worth as a divorced woman in a relationship with a man who wasn't her husband. Even if she was able to avoid those early morning whispers, I have to guess that she had voices in her head, hissing lies about who she was—just like so many of us do! But on that pivotal day in her life, when she bumped into Jesus at the well, her life was entirely redefined by the One she encountered.

Jesus is the One who speaks the truth about who I am and who you are. Social media doesn't tell us the truth. We're not defined by our work. Romantic partners don't determine our value. And whatever we like or don't like about our bodies cannot alter the reality that I am, and you are, God's beloved.

Perhaps, until now, you've owned the voices inside of your head. Instead, today listen for the voice of Jesus, telling you the *truth* about who you are.

QUESTIONS TO ASK YOURSELF

What are the lies—spoken aloud or swimming in my head—that I've believed?

What does Jesus have to say to that voice?

How can I practice stillness to make space for God to speak?

SCRIPTURE

THE WOMAN SAID,
"I KNOW THAT MESSIAH"
(CALLED CHRIST) IS COMING.
WHEN HE COMES, HE WILL
EXPLAIN EVERYTHING TO US."
THEN JESUS DECLARED,
"I, THE ONE SPEAKING
TO YOU—I AM HE."

—JOHN 4:25–26

PRAYER

God, You know me inside and out. You see the ways I've been bullied by the voices that tell me lies about who I am. I confess there are ways in which I've owned these voices. Forgive me. Help me to embrace the reality that, from all eternity, I have belonged to You. Expose every false idol in which I've placed my worth. Expose every lie and replace it with Your truth. Strengthen me to exercise patience, self-awareness, and persistence as You do Your work in me. I choose to embrace the fullness of my belovedness today.

AMEN.

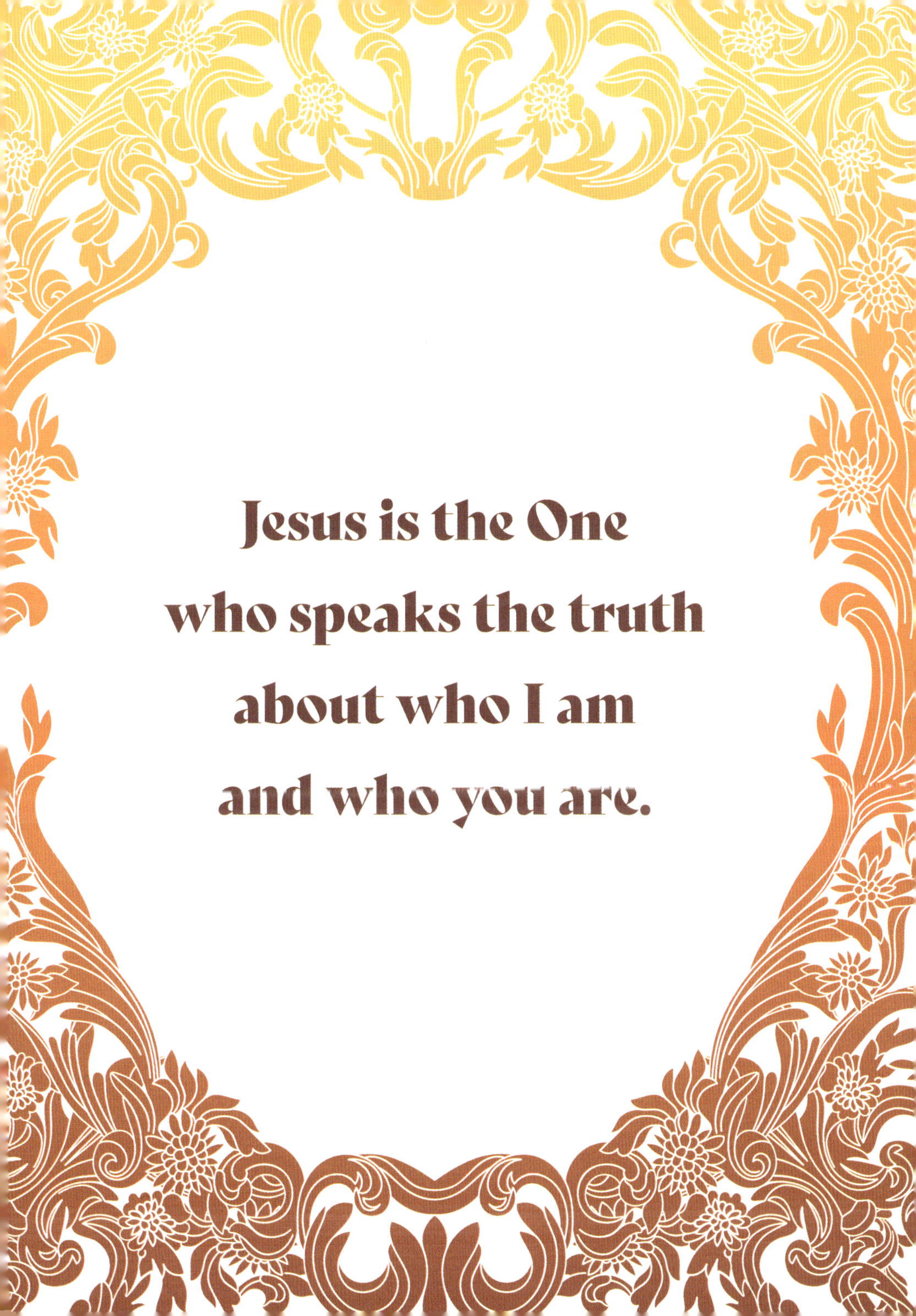
Jesus is the One
who speaks the truth
about who I am
and who you are.

You've owned the shame . . .

Belovedness

SARAH KROGER

0:18 3:42

THE POWER OF SHAME

Depending on what the situation called for, I spent most of my teenage years learning how to put on different masks. I donned the "peacemaker" mask whenever I sensed conflict—in my home, at my school, with my friends. I put on the "invisibility" mask when I wanted to stay under the radar rather than be noticed. And I'd show the world my "happy" mask when I was actually feeling tortured inside, but was terrified to admit it.

It's exhausting to wear masks, isn't it? For years, I struggled silently with crushing anxiety, ashamed to admit to anyone that I needed help. Not wanting to burden my family or friends with all I was carrying, I didn't know where to turn for help.

Where did keeping all of my pain secret land me? Suffering a panic attack the week after I graduated from high school, I wound up in the hospital. The precious façade I'd invested years into building, to fool those around me, had crumbled at my feet. I kept up the ruse, donning the masks as long as I could. Until I couldn't.

I was ashamed that I wasn't strong enough mentally or physically to navigate the chaotic world that my brain had become. When, at eighteen, I was diagnosed with severe anxiety and depression, I began taking medication. While I would have rather avoided the stigma I felt about taking it, therapy taught me that sometimes these things are just out of our control. And I became convinced that—on a chemical level!—the gift of modern medicine is often what God uses to heal our minds and bodies. I also discovered that having the support of others helped. Asking for help can actually be the strongest, bravest thing you can do when you need help.

At the end of Matthew's gospel, after the resurrection of Jesus, He appeared to His disciples. And before He returned to heaven to join His Father, He gave the disciples their marching orders: they were to make and baptize disciples (Matthew 28:19). And the promise Jesus made to His friends is the promise He makes to us as well: "I am with you always, to the very end of the age" (Matthew 28:20). We have confidence that even when we hide, Jesus is near.

Shame drives us into hiding, hissing into our ear that we're not good enough. Is there a way in which shame is bullying you? Maybe it's your mental health. Perhaps you've silently endured abuse. You may live with a disability. Or you may be concerned about the appearance of your body. Whatever challenge you're facing today, I encourage you to come out of hiding. You are worth caring for, and help is available. In addition to any medication your body may need, I encourage you to seek help from a therapist. If you don't know how to choose one, ask friends you trust. Your church may also offer a list of therapeutic professionals. In the same way God uses medicine to heal us, God can and does use these skilled professionals as agents of spiritual and emotional healing in our lives.

Beloved, this is how God transforms us. He uses His Word. He uses those who love us. He uses professional counselors. I know it takes courage to bring your shame into the light, but I promise that when you do, you will experience freedom.

QUESTIONS TO ASK YOURSELF

What is the shame that you're carrying, alone, today?

Who is one person you trust to support you?

What is one Scripture that empowers you to come out of hiding?

SCRIPTURE

THEN JESUS CAME TO THEM AND SAID, "ALL AUTHORITY IN HEAVEN AND ON EARTH HAS BEEN GIVEN TO ME. THEREFORE GO AND MAKE DISCIPLES OF ALL NATIONS, BAPTIZING THEM IN THE NAME OF THE FATHER AND OF THE SON AND OF THE HOLY SPIRIT, AND TEACHING THEM TO OBEY EVERYTHING I HAVE COMMANDED YOU. AND SURELY I AM WITH YOU ALWAYS, TO THE VERY END OF THE AGE."

—MATTHEW 28:18–20

PRAYER

Father, I turn to You as the One who created me and loves me. You are my Maker, and You know me inside and out. You know every accusing thought I've entertained, and You know the ones that have lodged in my deep places. Send Your Spirit to help me as I purpose to come out of hiding. Teach me, moment by moment, to discern the messages I've swallowed that are not from You. Then speak Your true Word to my heart and help me to claim and cling to what You have spoken. Father, I choose to believe that I am Yours, in this moment and all others. Teach me to live as Your Beloved child.

AMEN.

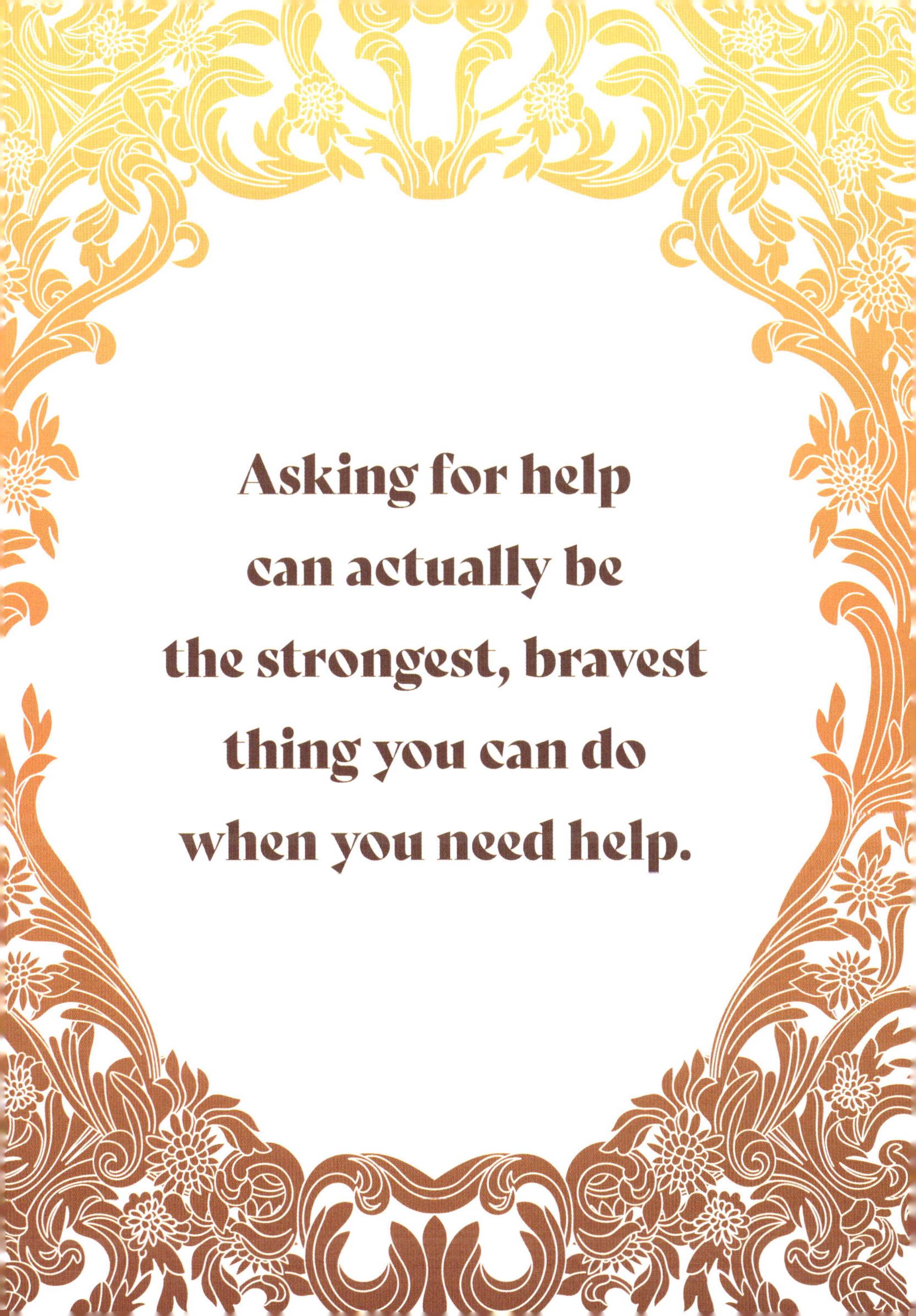
Asking for help
can actually be
the strongest, bravest
thing you can do
when you need help.

. . . and reproach of your failure. It's time to own your belovedness . . .

Belovedness

SARAH KROGER

0:21 3:42

LEARNING TO FAIL WELL

Early on in my career as an artist, I was invited to perform in Italy for an international music festival. It was the first time I had been hired to travel outside the country for music, and I was *thrilled*. An all-expenses-paid trip to Italy to sing my songs . . . what could be better for a twenty-three-year-old?! I spent a week in an adorable Italian village, judging songwriting competitions and meeting other artists from around the globe.

The main concert in which I would be performing was on the last night of the trip and I was so excited. This was my moment! That performance was the whole reason I'd been invited to participate at the festival.

The problem was that I wasn't prepared for how the Italian organizers put on shows. Even at that age, I felt relatively comfortable performing in the United States, but I didn't realize how different this would be. I was expected to walk around the stage, hitting marks in various spots, climbing up and down stairs filled with people. Honestly, it felt more like a Broadway musical number! All this to say, my vocal stamina was not up to par for such a spectacle, and

I had completely run out of air by the time the first chorus hit. For the remainder of the song, I looked and sounded like a struggling marathon runner at the end of their race. It was the worst performance of my life. An epic, total failure on an international stage. That was a long flight home.

Have you ever had a massive fail that just felt devastating? Maybe it was onstage, like me: a performance, or a speech, or a debate. Or maybe you humiliated yourself in front of others on an athletic playing field. Or your cringeworthy moment might have been a professional failure, when you didn't do what you were expected to do. These kinds of experiences can continue to impact us long after we've endured them.

I hate failing. I hate it so much that sometimes the fear of failure has held me back from starting a new endeavor. I allowed the sting of the previous failure to keep me stuck. But the older I get, the more I've been able to embrace failure as a gift. It's how we learn! It's how we figure out where we need to get stronger, where to focus our efforts. It keeps us humble. Besides, never failing doesn't mean you're doing great. In fact, if we never fail, we probably aren't pushing ourselves hard enough. Perfection isn't even possible, but progress absolutely is.

How can you learn from the last failure you experienced? How will you learn from your next one? I know it's a dramatic mind-shift to make, but I encourage you to make the choice to begin to embrace failure as a gift. When things go south—which they will for all of us from time to time!—pause to discern what you can learn and what you'll do differently the next time.

Failure has led me to grow in ways I never thought possible. I hope you'll consider looking at failure a little differently from now on.

QUESTIONS TO ASK YOURSELF

What is one way you failed when you were a child?

What is a recent failure you've experienced?

What can be learned from your failures?

SCRIPTURE

CONSIDER IT PURE JOY,
MY BROTHERS AND SISTERS,
WHENEVER YOU FACE TRIALS
OF MANY KINDS, BECAUSE YOU
KNOW THAT THE TESTING OF YOUR
FAITH PRODUCES PERSEVERANCE.
LET PERSEVERANCE FINISH ITS WORK
SO THAT YOU MAY
BE MATURE AND COMPLETE,
NOT LACKING ANYTHING.

—JAMES 1:2-4

PRAYER

God, I thank You that I belong to You. You know my heart, and so You know that I would rather win than lose. I'd rather succeed than fail. And I'll admit that I am afraid to fail! I confess that my past failures have kept me stuck at times, fearful about moving forward. Father, I offer it all to You. I entrust my failures to You and ask You to give me courage to do all that You've called me to do. When I fail, give me Your vision to learn from my mistakes so that I might grow. Thank You for all the opportunities You've put before me. Give me the courage to say yes!

AMEN.

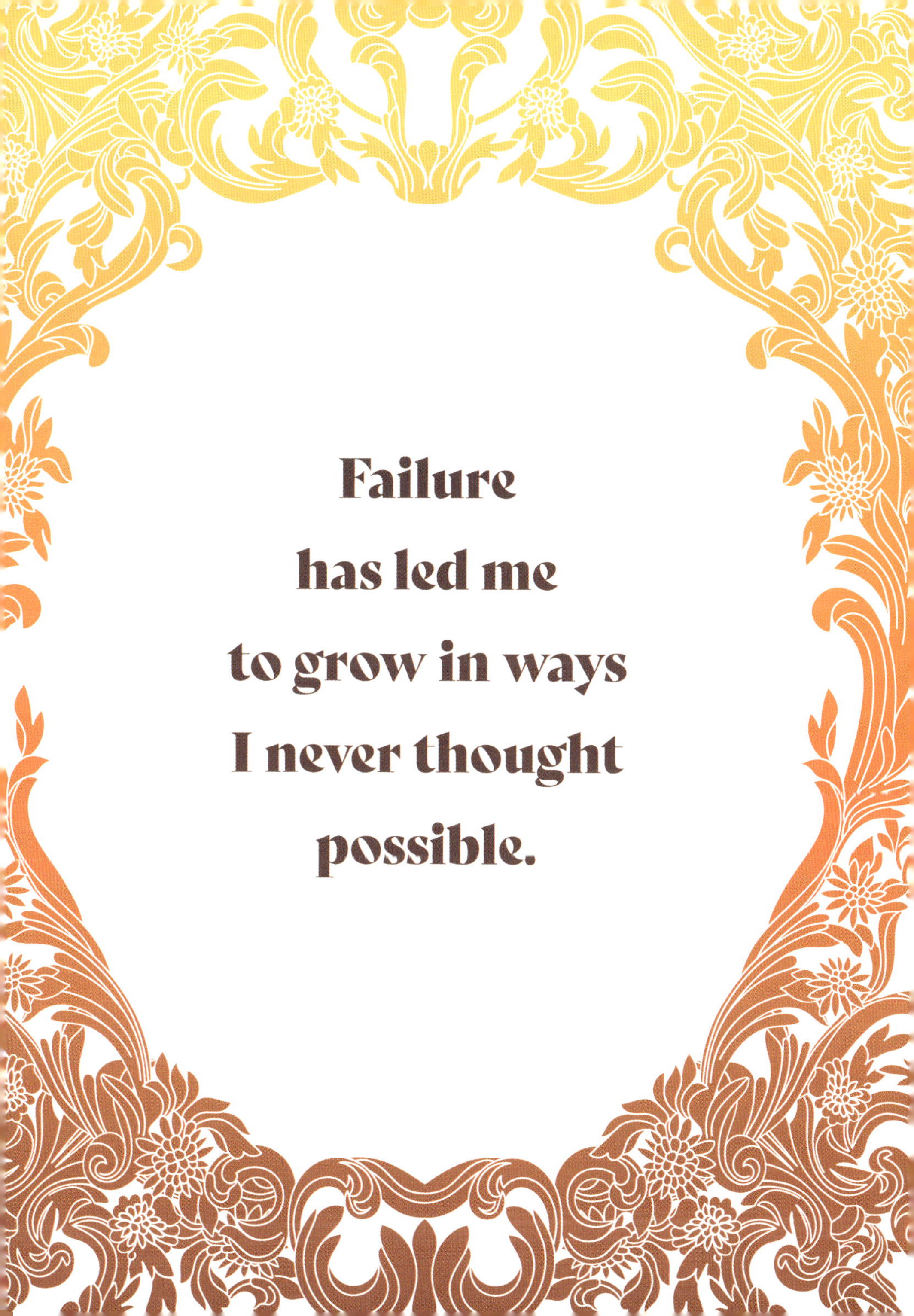
Failure
has led me
to grow in ways
I never thought
possible.

You've owned your past...

Belovedness

SARAH KROGER

0:31 3:42

DEFINED BY LOVE

My sister and I had taken our baths and put on our pajamas. We were curled up in our blankets, watching reruns of *I Love Lucy*. Somber, our parents muted the TV and asked us to sit with them on the couch. The meeting felt familiar. A year earlier, they'd gathered us to tell us that they were separating. I recognized the same look on their faces. And now, a year later, they told us they had decided it was time for them to get a divorce. I was ten years old, and life as I knew it came crashing down around me.

I don't think you ever truly "get over" your parents getting divorced. Yes, the wound has turned into a scar over time, but the scar will always be there. No matter how friendly everyone remains, you can't help but think about it at family gatherings, during big life changes—like getting married or having kids of your own—during the holidays, etc. And when you endure divorce as a child, you have no control. You have no choice. It's something that happens to you, and you're simply expected to get with the program.

There were times early on, in my childhood, when I allowed the wound of divorce to define me. Those were the times when I believed that because I had come from a broken home, I was broken—and I was destined to remain so forever. And if I was broken, perhaps everything I touched would break too. Thankfully, after years of healing through therapy, as well as the love of God and others, I'm now able to see the divorce as just one piece of my story. It doesn't define me, just like the bullying I experienced when I was young doesn't define me. Just like my failures don't define me. Just like my sin doesn't define me. They are all simply pieces of the story of Sarah Kroger's beautiful and messy life.

When I consider my own wounds and weaknesses, I can't help but think of the words of Saint Pope John Paul II that have meant so much to me over the years. He said, "We are not the sum of our weaknesses and failures; we are the sum of the Father's love for us and our real capacity to become the image of His Son, Jesus."

Do you believe that? Not just in your head, but in your heart? In your bones? The most real and true thing about you has nothing to do with what's happened to you. It doesn't even have to do with the choices you've made, good or bad. The most real and true thing about who you are is the Father's steadfast, unfailing love for you.

What could be different about your life if you chose to be defined by the Father's love for you? I'm guessing that the hurts of your past—the neglect, the absence, the loss—wouldn't have as much power to bully you. None of the pieces of your beautiful and messy life can define you without your permission. So, as you are being transformed into the image of Jesus, your purpose is to live as one who is defined by the Father's love.

Today, I am no longer owned by my past. And you don't have to be either.

QUESTIONS TO ASK YOURSELF

Is there an experience from your past that still haunts you today?

I invite you to reflect on the question I posed earlier in this chapter: What could be different about your life if you chose to be defined by the Father's love for you?

SCRIPTURE

"FOR GOD
SO LOVED THE WORLD
THAT HE GAVE HIS
ONE AND ONLY SON, THAT
WHOEVER BELIEVES IN HIM
SHALL NOT PERISH
BUT HAVE ETERNAL LIFE."

—JOHN 3:16

PRAYER

Precious Father, thank You for loving me with a perfect love. I'm so grateful that I am not defined by what has happened to me. I cannot even be defined by the mistakes I've made. Today I choose to embrace the reality that, above everything else, I am defined by Your love. I surrender my past to Your mercy. I lay my future in Your hands. Guide my steps as I try my best to follow You.

AMEN.

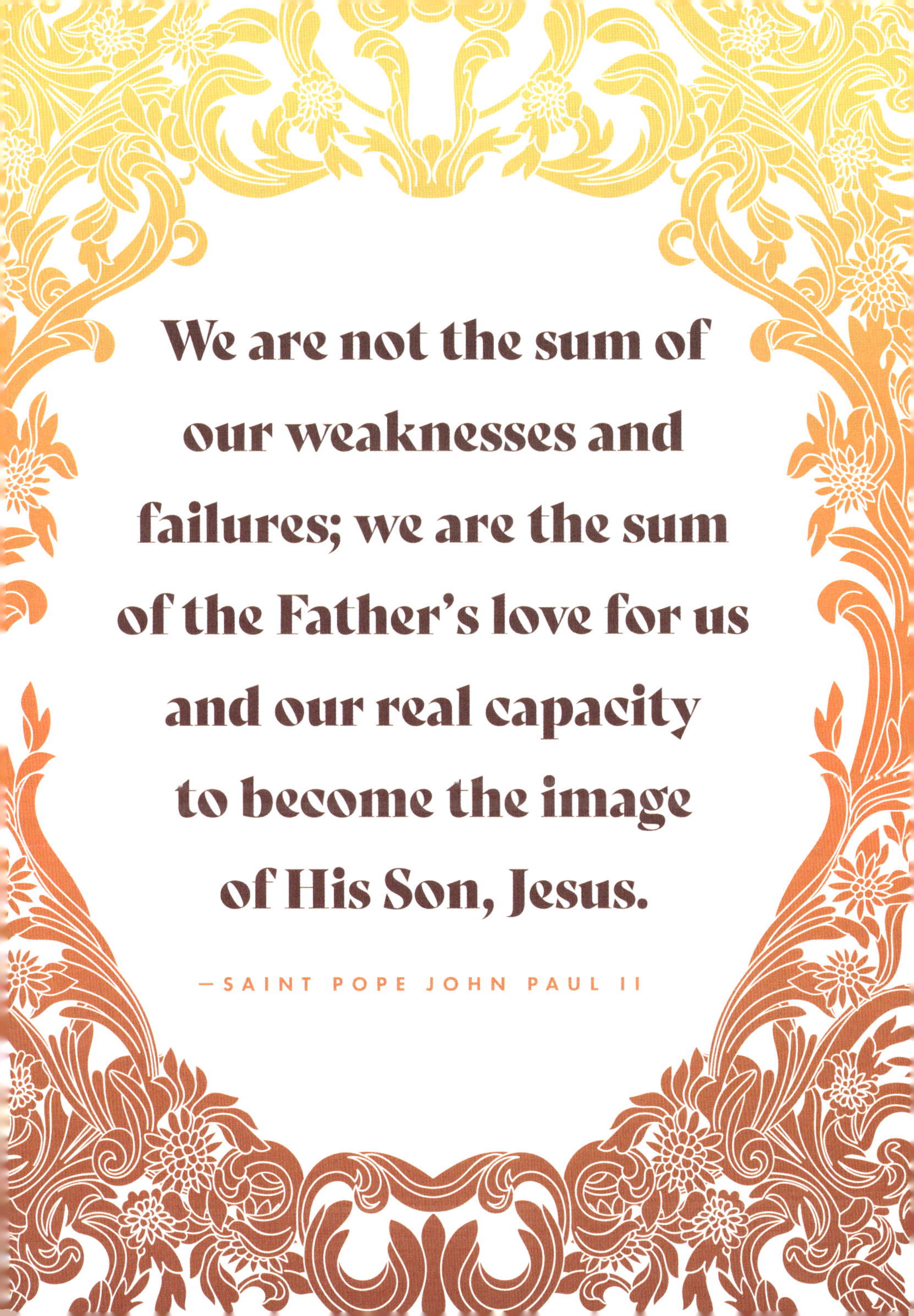

We are not the sum of our weaknesses and failures; we are the sum of the Father's love for us and our real capacity to become the image of His Son, Jesus.

—SAINT POPE JOHN PAUL II

. . . and how it's defined you . . .

Belovedness

SARAH KROGER

0:33 3:42

WANTING TO BE WHO I'M NOT

When I was coming up as a songwriter, I didn't have a church environment where I could be mentored in songwriting or in leading worship. And so I'd often look toward other artists and worship leaders around the country to inspire and educate me . . . artists like Matt Maher, Kari Jobe, or Christy Nockels. I'd watch them lead worship, and they became my teachers.

But instead of just learning from them, I began to compare myself to them every time I went onstage. And the looping tape of negativity would start scrolling in my head. The lying voice would start hissing that I wasn't enough. *If I don't lead like they do, I'm not doing it right. I must not be doing a good job.*

You can't compare your first year on the job to someone else's tenth year, nor your gifting to anyone else's. In fact, Saint Paul said in his letter to the Corinthians (I Corinthians chapter 12) that when you are trying to let the Spirit of God work through you, jealousy has no place, and it makes no sense. It would be like the eye being jealous of the ear, or the hand saying to the foot, "I don't need you." They both have an essential role.

If we cannot appreciate the belovedness of others, we will not be able to appreciate our own belovedness. If we are convinced that someone else's giftedness takes away from our own, then we have seriously underestimated the Giver.

I wasn't made to be Christy Nockels.

I wasn't made to be Matt Maher.

I wasn't made to be Kari Jobe.

I was made to be Sarah Kroger. I was made to reflect the glory of God in my own unique way.

Comparison is something I've battled on and off for years, but it all came to a head during the COVID-19 pandemic. When I no longer had opportunities to lead worship like before, I found myself in what I now call a season of *pruning*. When vine growers prune plants, they cut the plant back further than you'd expect. For example, a once-lush fig tree might get pruned to look like a stump with a few bare branches. At first glance, you might question whether it was ever going to grow back. But in fact, by pruning it well, the branches come back even stronger! The fruit is more vibrant and beautiful.

During the pandemic, I felt like life and ministry as I knew it was being pruned in a way that felt very scary. I didn't know if it would ever come back again. I was no longer able to wrap my identity up in my work. I wasn't able to compare myself to anyone. It simply became about what God was calling me to do and who He was calling me to be.

He wasn't calling me to be anyone other than who I am. God has always been inviting me to be *Sarah Kroger*. He has called me to do what He has chosen *me* to do. Nouwen shares, "When I write to you that, as the Beloved, we are God's chosen ones, I mean that we have been seen by God from all eternity and seen as unique, special, precious beings."[3] Not only are we made uniquely by God, but we are seen and known by Him.

My past had bullied me into believing I had to be like others in order to be loved or accepted, but God revealed that I was made by Him—unique, special, precious—to be and to do what only I can.

I entered a rebuilding phase where my calling and ministry grew back so much stronger than it was before. I've never felt more peaceful and free as a worship leader, as a songwriter, as a child of God. I love who He's made *me* to be, rather than trying to be someone else. I was finally able to see that it's never been about how good I am. It's always been about how good He is. And all this time, God was inviting me to reflect that goodness in my own beautiful way to the world.

God is inviting you to be and to do what *only you* can.

---

3. Nouwen, *Life of the Beloved*, 53.

QUESTIONS TO ASK YOURSELF

Who is someone you've compared yourself to?

Have you ever experienced a season of "pruning"? Or is God inviting you into a season of pruning today?

SCRIPTURE

“ARE NOT TWO SPARROWS
SOLD FOR A PENNY?
YET NOT ONE OF THEM
WILL FALL TO THE GROUND
OUTSIDE YOUR FATHER’S CARE.
AND EVEN THE VERY HAIRS OF
YOUR HEAD ARE ALL NUMBERED.
SO DON’T BE AFRAID;
YOU ARE WORTH MORE THAN
MANY SPARROWS.”

—MATTHEW 10:29–31

PRAYER

Creator God, You are so good. I praise You, and I ask You to help me embrace the truth that I am fearfully and wonderfully made. I confess that I have compared myself to others. Father, fill me with a holy boldness to embrace exactly who You've made me to be. And give me vision to notice and affirm the ways that others are entirely unique and special because of who You are and what You've done in them.

AMEN.

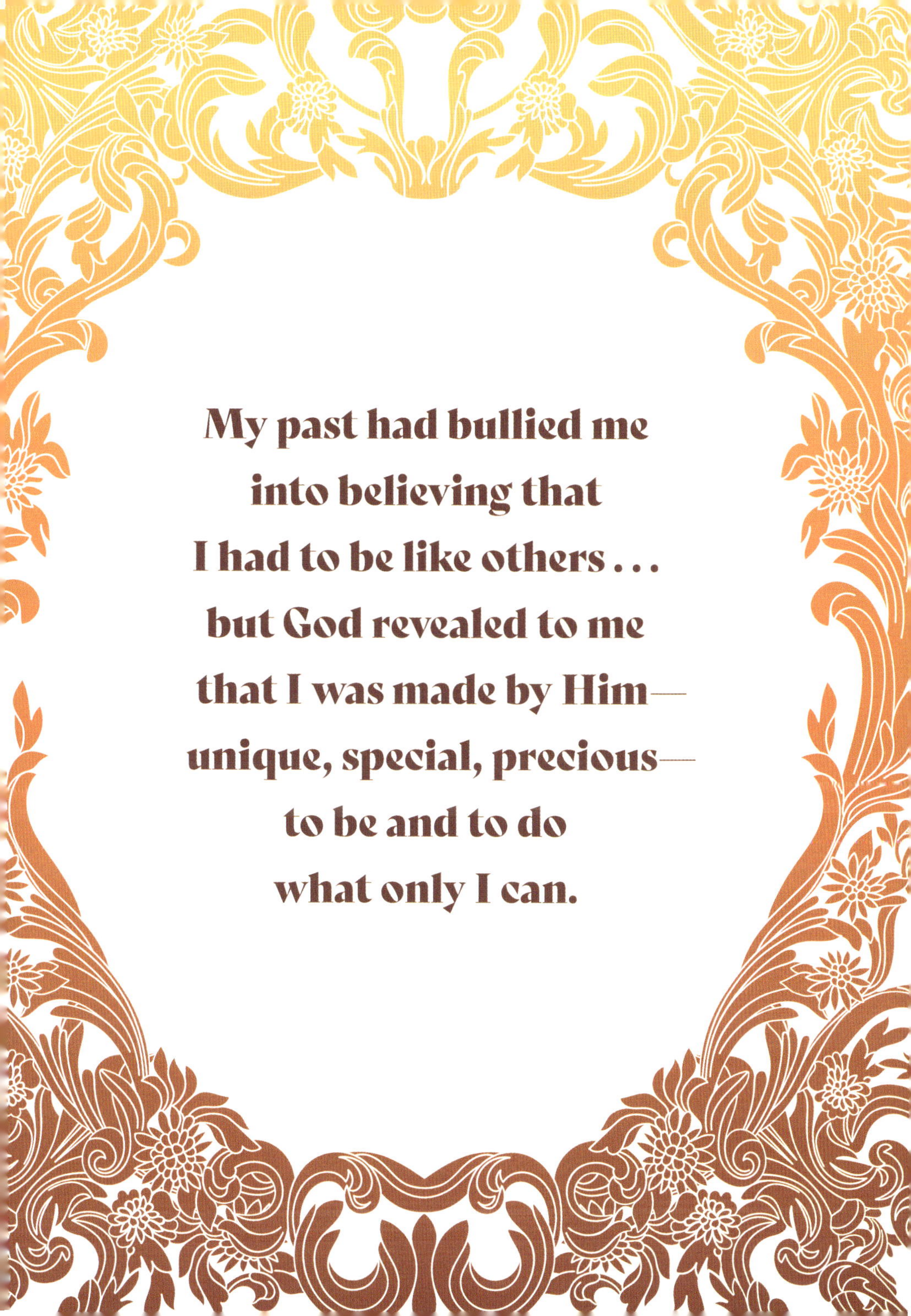

My past had bullied me
into believing that
I had to be like others . . .
. . . but God revealed to me
that I was made by Him—
unique, special, precious—
to be and to do
what only I can.

You've owned everything everybody else says . . .

Belovedness

SARAH KROGER

0:35 3:42

WHAT OTHER PEOPLE SAY

Most jobs involve some sort of regular evaluation or review with a boss. When your job requires being in the "public eye," the criticism tends to be sharper and crueler. I understand that it comes with the territory. Still, it can be a little jarring when people who don't know you at all make public comments about you. And even in a sea of lovely compliments and engaged fans, it's strangely easier to focus on the nasty critiques and unimpressed faces.

I've had plenty of negative things said about me. I'm sure you've had something negative said about you. These days, I mostly let them go in one ear and out the other. But it wasn't always like that.

Do you know those moments in life when everything changes?

That happened for me when I was twenty-nine. I had been married just over a year when a friend recommended that little book I mentioned earlier by Henri Nouwen called *Life of the Beloved.* I can still see where I was sitting—on the balcony of our downtown Roswell apartment—as I started reading it for the first time. In one of the passages that was paradigm-shifting for me, Nouwen describes the way God speaks to us, explaining, "Yes, there is that voice, the voice that speaks from above and from within and that whispers softly or declares loudly: 'You are my Beloved, on you my favor rests.'"[4] It's beautiful, right? I think that hearing those words—"You are My Beloved"—is what we were made for. It's what we hunger for.

We hear God speak these very words in the Bible at the baptism of Jesus. Jesus's cousin John was baptizing people when Jesus came to be baptized as well. He was around thirty years old, and about to launch His public ministry. When Jesus was being baptized by John, those who had gathered saw what looked like a dove descending on Him, and they heard God's voice. That Voice from heaven announced, "You are My Son, whom I love; with You I am well pleased" (Luke 3:22).

The words that God spoke to Jesus are the words He also speaks to us:

You are Mine.

I love you.

Even Jesus took a moment to have the voice of God define Him before the rest of the world could. In a society with a myriad of voices eager to tell us who we are, we desperately need to hear the Voice that is true.

Nouwen says, "It certainly is not easy to hear that voice in a

---

4. Nouwen, *Life of the Beloved*, 30–31.

world filled with voices that shout: 'You are no good, you are ugly; you are worthless; you are despicable, you are nobody—unless you can demonstrate the opposite.'"[5]

How did he just get inside my head?!

Tears filled my eyes. I remember putting the book down and thinking, *God is speaking directly to me.* It felt like a light bulb had just turned on. From that moment, I was set on a different path.

I would start training myself to listen to the still, strong voice at the center of my being that was, and is, whispering, *You are My beloved.* As I held Nouwen's book in my hands, I began to imagine a world in which I really could live from the truth instead of from the noise.

I still get criticized from time to time. Heck, sometimes I deserve it. Not *every* negative comment is untrue. But I'm not looking for approval or acceptance from critics—I only wish to be pleasing to God.

Am I doing the best I can with what I've been given? If so, I can be at peace.

5. Nouwen, *Life of the Beloved*, 31.

QUESTIONS TO ASK YOURSELF

Are you able to hear the kind Voice of the Father speaking over you?

What makes it harder for you to believe that you are God's Beloved?

What do you need to eliminate from your life to *live* as the Beloved?

SCRIPTURE

WHEN ALL THE PEOPLE
WERE BEING BAPTIZED,
JESUS WAS BAPTIZED TOO.
AND AS HE WAS PRAYING,
HEAVEN WAS OPENED AND
THE HOLY SPIRIT DESCENDED ON HIM
IN BODILY FORM LIKE A DOVE.
AND A VOICE CAME FROM HEAVEN:
"YOU ARE MY SON, WHOM I LOVE;
WITH YOU I AM WELL PLEASED."

—LUKE 3:21–22

PRAYER

Lord, I thank You that You are continually making Yourself known to me. Your heart is so kind and faithful. Not for a moment have I left Your sight. You are closer to me than the air I'm breathing. Silence the noise. Open the ears of my heart so that I can hear You clearly when You speak Your love to me. Father, I trust in Your great love for me.

AMEN.

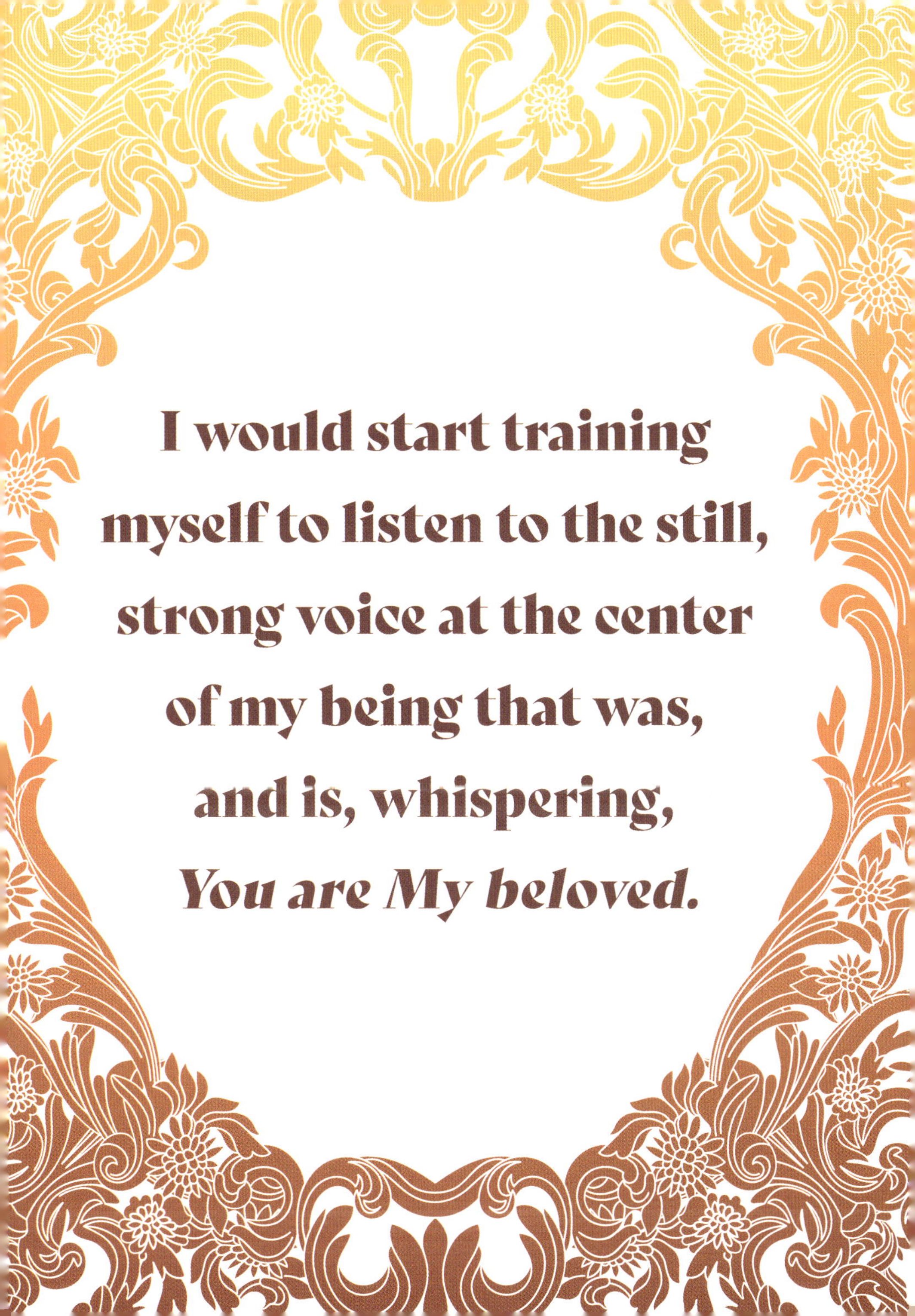
I would start training
myself to listen to the still,
strong voice at the center
of my being that was,
and is, whispering,
You are My beloved.

From all eternity, from long before you were born and became a part of history, you existed in God's heart.

–HENRI NOUWEN

It's time to hear what your Father has spoken. It's time to own your belovedness . . .

Belovedness

SARAH KROGER

0:41 3:42

WHAT YOUR FATHER HAS SPOKEN

If you have a gift you know is from God and you aren't sharing it, you're denying the glory of God within you."

I was sixteen, attending a youth camp that would prove to be incredibly formative in my life, when I heard those words from the stage. I think they were so impactful because it was the first time I realized that my participation in faith was about more than checking off the boxes. It was more than following a set of rules. As a result of that week at camp, I began to understand that Jesus is real. Jesus is a real person who wants a relationship with me and I with Him. I realized that He cared about everything in my life, every decision I was making. But the pivotal moment of that week for me was when that speaker challenged us to use the gifts that God had given us: "If you have a gift you know is from God and you aren't sharing it, you're denying the glory of God within you."

I started to consider the gift that might be in me. Specifically, I began to imagine using my voice. Up until that point, I had let fear get in the way of allowing God to use it. Fear of judgment, fear of being made fun of, fear of failing. Music quickly became the way I prayed. It was how I communed with God. After that week at camp, I started singing at church voluntarily (rather than being forced to by my musical parents). I started to say yes when I was invited to lead worship, and I started to embrace my voice as a gift. Was I still afraid? Absolutely. It wasn't like I woke up one day and all the fear was gone. I was afraid to sing in front of people. I would literally shake from head to toe, even sounding like some kind of dying animal every time I stepped up to the microphone. It wasn't great for a very long time. But I kept showing up because I was convinced that God was asking me to do it. I was convicted that the gift God had given me wasn't meant just for me. And little by little, my confidence grew.

What is the gift inside of you that's not yet being shared? Maybe you already know. You might be convinced that God has called you to pursue the sciences because your brain is wired to understand complex principles and apply what you learn to new experiments. Or maybe you have the gift of caring for those with unique needs. Or maybe the gift inside you is similar to the one inside me; you delight in creating with music, or fabric, or words, or paint, or clay.

Beloved, sometimes the enemy tries to convince us that God has not spoken and God is not speaking. But it's simply not true. God's assurance to His people through Jeremiah is the same promise God makes to us today: "Call to Me and I will answer you and tell you great and unsearchable things you do not know" (Jeremiah 33:3). It's a big promise, right? It is. And it's time to hear what your Father has spoken.

Through a leader onstage with a microphone, I heard God inviting me to use the gifts that He had placed in me. Someone else might hear God speaking to them through a trusted advisor or guide. And another person will hear God speaking clearly to them through prayer or the pages of Scripture. Each of these experiences is a unique thread in the tapestry of our faith journeys, weaving together a message of divine love and purpose.

It's time to start hearing and accepting God's love for you, recognizing that He is reaching out in ways that are as diverse as our individual paths. Embrace the ways He communicates with you, and let that love transform your heart, guiding you toward a deeper understanding of your own worth and the impact you can make in the world.

QUESTIONS TO ASK YOURSELF

Have you experienced a time when you felt
compelled to share your gifts?

What is one gift—a skill, an interest, a passion—
God has given you?

How is God asking you
to share your gifts with the world today?

SCRIPTURE

"CALL TO ME AND
I WILL ANSWER YOU AND
TELL YOU GREAT AND
UNSEARCHABLE THINGS
YOU DO NOT KNOW."

—JEREMIAH 33:3

PRAYER

Lord, I thank You that from the moment You created me, You have been with me. You have been near. Today I am leaning in toward the sound of Your voice. Help me to listen and respond to what You are calling me to do. I surrender my gifts to You. I give You my "yes" in this moment. Father, You know my heart. You know the ways I've been bound by fear, and I believe You are setting me free. Give me a bold confidence in You. Set me free from any fear that holds me back. I am Yours, and I believe You are at work in me and through me.

AMEN.

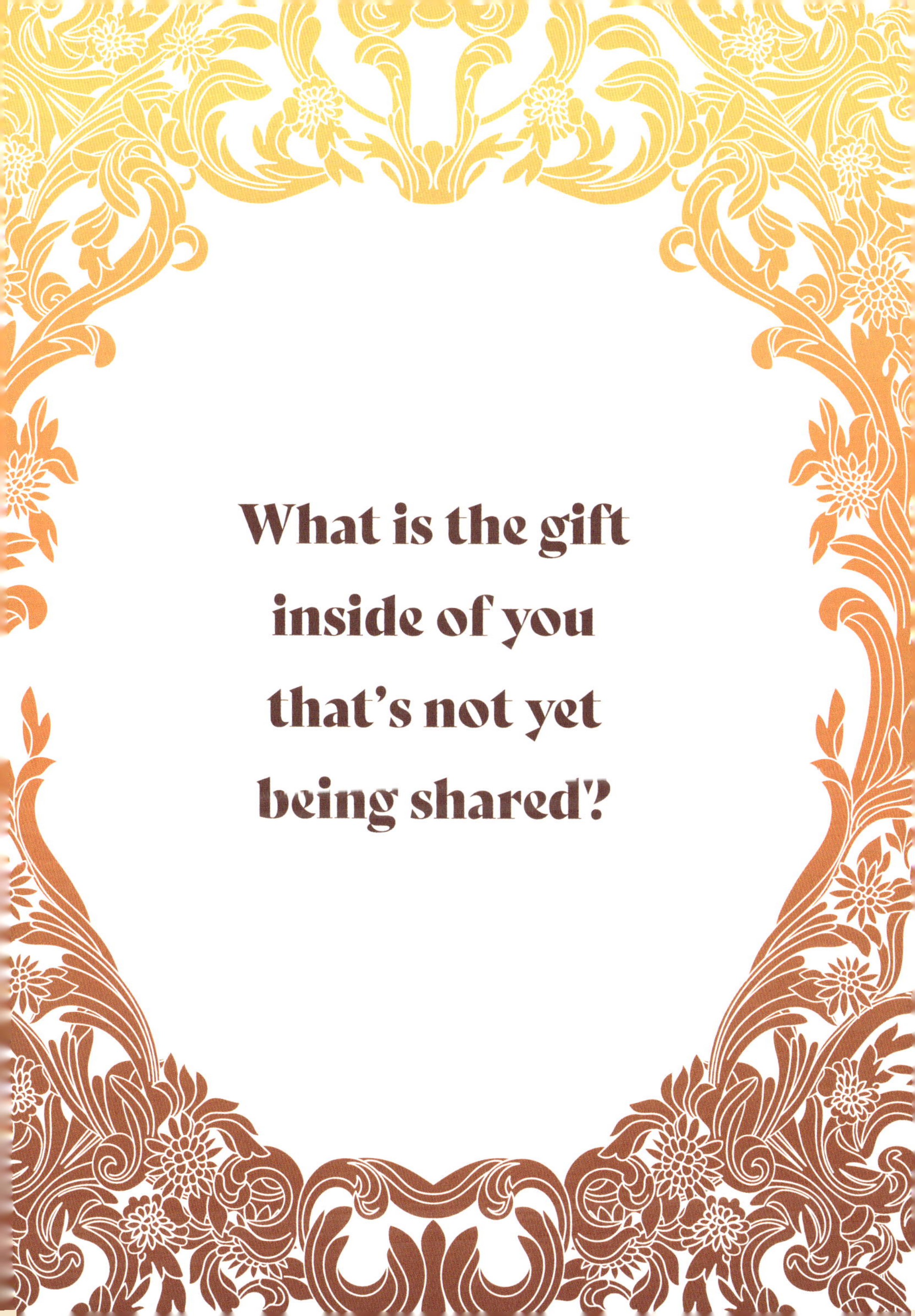

What is the gift inside of you that's not yet being shared?

He says,
"You're
Mine..."

Belovedness

SARAH KROGER

0:53 3:42

YOU ARE MINE

Remember those chalky pastel hearts you handed out to classmates with your store-bought Valentines? They really didn't have much taste, but each one bore a sweet sentiment:

Cutie Pie	*UR Cute*	*Hug Me*
Kiss Me	*Be True*	*Beloved*
XOXO	*Love You*	*I Like You*

Wouldn't it be nice if hearing from God was as easy as receiving a candy heart? Or unfolding a message from a fortune cookie? Or receiving a note sent by carrier pigeon?

While it's not quite that simple, God does speak to our hearts.

Through the story that unfolds in the Old Testament, we arrive at a moment when God's people were struggling. They'd been thrust into exile, scattered far from home. Their trust was fading. Many wrestled to believe that God was still with them and for them.

Maybe you know what that's like. Maybe you know what it's like to be away from home, yearning for stability. Hungry to hear a loving voice. Lonely for the One who loves you perfectly.

Maybe you felt alone the first time you went to camp.

Or you felt disoriented your first week away at college.

Maybe you've lost someone you love, or a relationship has

ended, and you are currently experiencing what it feels like to be entirely undone.

When God's people were in exile, far from home, they lost their sense of identity. They began to turn to other people and things besides God for their sense of worth and purpose. But God spoke hope to them through the prophet Isaiah:

> *"Do not fear, for I have redeemed you; I have summoned you by name; you are Mine. When you pass through the waters, I will be with you; and when you pass through the rivers, they will not sweep over you. When you walk through the fire, you will not be burned . . . since you are precious and honored in My sight, and because I love you."* —Isaiah 43:1–2, 4

In this comforting message of assurance, God speaks the words that every human heart is hungry to hear:

Do not fear.

You are Mine.

I will be with you.

You are precious.

I love you.

(I mean, this guy could really make it big in the candy-heart business, am I right?)

Beloved, God is faithful to speak directly to our hearts in a way that we can understand. Do you see how He calmed His people's fears and reminded them of their identity? "You are Mine" is neither aggressive nor possessive. It's a Fatherly reminder that He is invested in us, and we do not need to fear being abandoned.

I heard God speaking through a book written by a stranger halfway around the world who somehow understood the specific struggles I was facing. God spoke to His ancient people through His servant Isaiah. Today, we can hear God's voice speaking to us through Scripture or the words of someone in our lives who knows and loves us. We might even hear God through a message on a candy heart.

What I want you to know is that God is *still* speaking and you *can* hear Him. He does not play games with us by hiding from us. God *is* speaking in a way you can discern and understand.

That said, His voice may not be *loud*. In fact, very rarely does God speak using a loud, thunderous voice from the heavens. More often, God's voice is gentle. Remember in I Kings 19, the Lord wasn't in the earthquake or the fire, the snapping trees or the crashing rocks. He made Himself known in a still, quiet whisper.

You can be sure that, in every moment, God's still, small voice is whispering to your heart, *You're Mine. Listen.*

QUESTIONS TO ASK YOURSELF

Do you believe that God is at work for your greatest good?

Was there ever a season when you struggled, needing to know God was near? Tell the story.

When you hear God call you "Beloved," are you able to receive that true word?

SCRIPTURE

"DO NOT FEAR, FOR I HAVE
REDEEMED YOU; I HAVE SUMMONED
YOU BY NAME; YOU ARE MINE.
WHEN YOU PASS THROUGH THE WATERS,
I WILL BE WITH YOU; AND WHEN YOU
PASS THROUGH THE RIVERS,
THEY WILL NOT SWEEP OVER YOU.
WHEN YOU WALK THROUGH THE FIRE,
YOU WILL NOT BE BURNED. . . .
SINCE YOU ARE PRECIOUS
AND HONORED IN MY SIGHT,
AND BECAUSE I LOVE YOU."

—ISAIAH 43:1–2, 4

PRAYER

God, help me to believe, deep in my heart, that You don't hide from me. You made me, and I am Yours. When I sit in stillness, working to silence the voices that speak lies, help me to hear You. Help me to hear You saying, "You are Mine." I am Yours when I pass through the waters. I am Yours when I'm struggling in the valley. I am Yours when I walk through the fire. Today I am owning what is most true: I am Yours. No matter what. Thank You for Your love that is available to me in every moment. You are my rock, and I receive the love You have for me. Because of Your love, I reject fear. Because of Your love, I am entirely secure.

AMEN.

God is faithful
to speak directly
to our hearts
in a way that
we can understand.

Belovedness

SARAH KROGER

0:56 3:42

FROM THE BEGINNING

Slim remnants of spaghetti and broccoli are left on four plates at our dining room table. I'm eight years old. While my dad is running through the house, waving a red tablecloth like the French flag, my mom, sister, and I are singing "One Day More" from *Les Miserables* at the top of our lungs, imitating the various characters in the show, using different voices and accents. Had someone knocked on the door, they might naturally have assumed we were rehearsing for some production. Nope. It was just a regular night at the Kroger household, where it was common for us to be belting out show tunes at dinnertime. *Les Mis* was one of our favorites, but *The Little Mermaid* and *Beauty and the Beast* were right up there too.

God had *made me* to sing.

But because of all the bullying I experienced in elementary school, I wanted to keep my self-expression hidden. Singing makes a person vulnerable, and the thought of being vulnerable in front of other people in that way was terrifying.

I did, however, love to sing in the privacy of our backyard. I'd put on my little Walkman, with matching headphones, and be transported to another world. I'd physically be on the play structure in the backyard, but in my mind I was performing onstage with Faith Hill singing my heart out to "This Kiss."

I didn't yet know that God had *made me* to sing. I didn't know that God had carefully crafted me together in my mother's womb—with a purpose and for a purpose. I didn't know that when God was knitting me together, dreaming of the Sarah I'd one day become, He was smiling. God was *delighting* in me.

Have you ever looked at the faces of brand-new parents? They are beaming! They delight in their child and find that baby to be incredible. Magnificent. That is a reflection of how God delights in us as His children. Sometimes we get little tastes of that delight on this side of heaven. For me, that foretaste has come through the face of my dear husband. He *delights* in me.

It's so different from what we see when we look at ourselves in the mirror, isn't it? We tend to notice all the things we are not. But when God looks at us, He sees who we *are*. He sees who He made us to be. He knows every detail of us, from head to toe. Not a single part of who we are is a mistake.

When you begin to live in this reality, everything changes. When you choose to believe what is most true, it starts to soak into your deepest places. Nouwen explains, "Long before any human being saw us, we are seen by God's loving eyes. Long before anyone heard us cry or laugh, we are heard by our God who is all ears for us. Long before any person spoke to us in the world, we are spoken to by the voice of eternal love. Our preciousness, uniqueness, and individuality are not given to us by those who need us in clock time, but by the One who has chosen us with an everlasting love, a love that existed from all eternity and will last through all eternity."[6]

Beloved, He has called you by name. You are His. Maybe you've heard that a thousand times or maybe this is the first time you've heard it. I pray it would resonate with you and sink deep into your bones so you can see how God sees you—as His beloved child. This has been true from the beginning. God's love for you was established before you could do anything to earn it or to lose it.

Tonight, before you drift off to sleep, close your eyes and imagine God knitting you together in your mother's womb. Then notice the smile of the One who delights in who He made you to be.

6. Nouwen, *Life of the Beloved*, 58.

QUESTIONS TO ASK YOURSELF

When you were a child, what brought you joy?

What's that thing you sense God has created you to do?

Can you see God's face *delighting* in you? Why or why not?

SCRIPTURE

"BEFORE I FORMED YOU
IN THE WOMB I KNEW YOU,
BEFORE YOU WERE BORN
I SET YOU APART;
I APPOINTED YOU AS
A PROPHET TO THE NATIONS."

—JEREMIAH 1:5

PRAYER

God of all creation, show me Your face. Show me the face that delights in me and delights in each person You've carefully crafted. Lord, I confess that it's easier to imagine a face that's disappointed or angry than one that delights in who I am. By Your Spirit, show Yourself to me. Thank You for the careful, intentional way You fashioned me. Give me eyes to see how I can continue to become who You have made me to be. I trust that You are present, that You are close, and that You are "all ears." Moment by moment, help me to walk in the reality that I am Your beloved child.

AMEN.

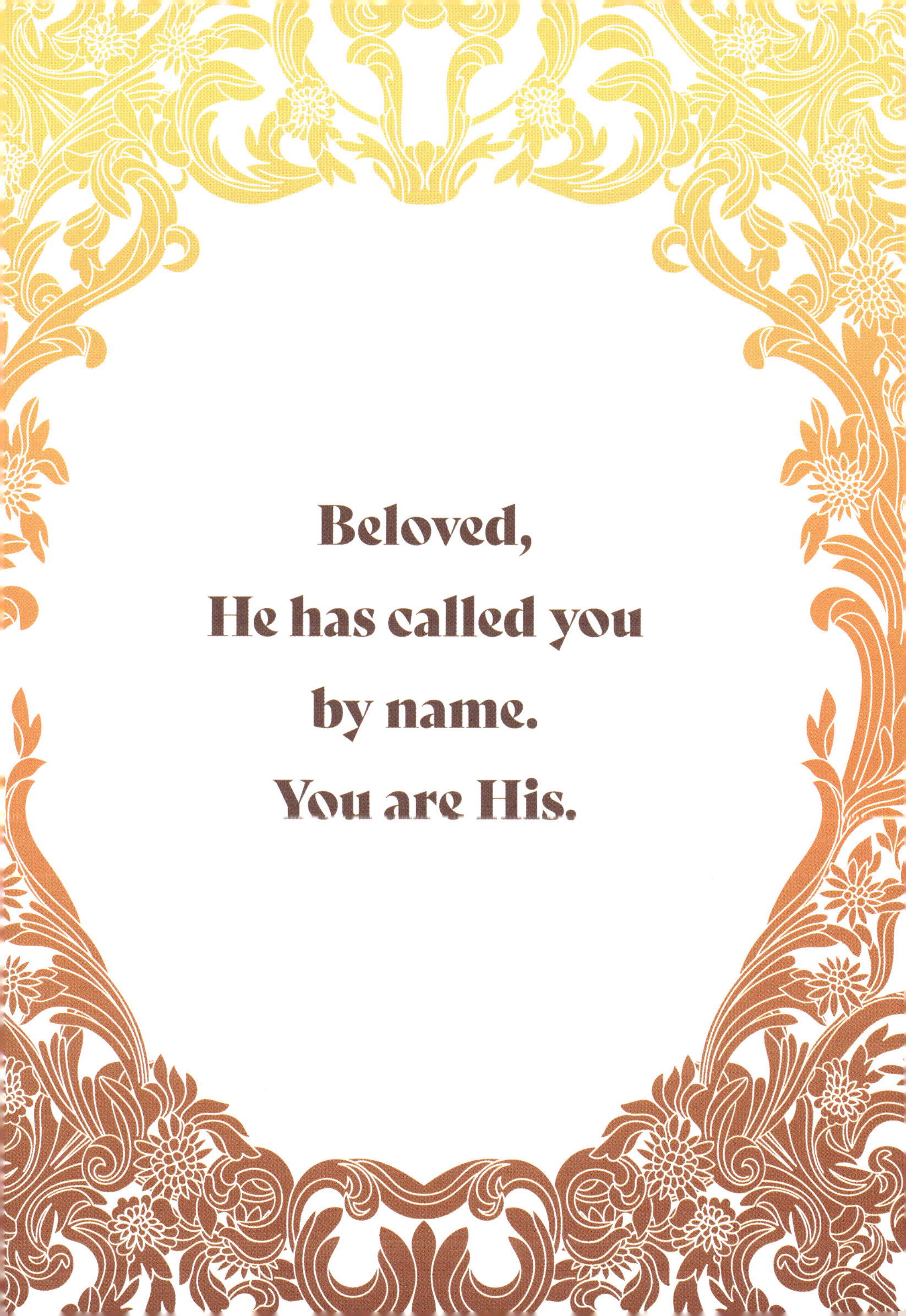
Beloved,
He has called you
by name.
You are His.

I find you beautiful in every way...

Belovedness

SARAH KROGER

0:58 3:42

OH, HOW BEAUTIFUL

"You look beautiful, babe."

As we were getting ready to go out to dinner, my husband's innocent remark touched something inside me. I was tempted to resist, to protest. Glancing in the mirror, I tried to see what he saw. And—because God had been working on my heart—I *did* see what he saw.

For years, I had seen something very different. What I saw when I looked in the mirror was the little girl who had been called a "dork." I'd judge my nose. I'd be disappointed in my thinning hair. I'd wish that my skinny "chicken legs" had some more meat on the bone.

My husband's words weren't the first time I'd received a compliment. Whenever my friends said something kind about me, I'd say, "Stop, you're just being nice." Inside I'd be thinking, *You don't really mean that.* I heard their words, but I never *received* them.

Everyone has insecurities regardless of how talented or celebrated or "conventionally attractive" they may be. What are we judging ourselves against, exactly? The unique characteristics that you or I have are part of what makes us human. You could call them flaws or imperfections, but I see the same brilliant diversity and design in a group of people as I do in a field of wildflowers. If you look closely, each one is different—not flawed. They aren't "perfect." But the Designer is perfect, and they reflect His boundless creativity.

Once I finally came to believe that I was God's beloved, I began to notice how negative and harmful that self-talk was inside my head. And as God's Spirit opened my ears to hear it, I had to make a choice. Would I continue to cling to the lies that were familiar, or would I listen to the voice that was speaking God's truth? As I let God transform my heart and my mind, I was able to choose the truth more readily, more often.

We all have these things, right? We see ourselves one way, and we wrestle to see the beauty and the goodness that others see in us. So, when they name what is true, it can feel jarring for our insides. We resist.

But you can make the decision to silence the lies. You can get with God in prayer and ask Him to speak truth to you through His Word. You might choose to invite a spiritual director to guide you on the journey. You might enlist a therapist to help you as you navigate this road to freedom, and you can choose to trust the words of the people in your life who know you and love you. If you struggle to believe that God finds you beautiful in every way, you're not alone.

All of us are bombarded, daily, by messages that insist otherwise:

God is absent.

What you have to offer isn't valuable.

You are ugly.

The enemy speaks—shouts!—lies. When you hear them, I challenge you to tip your ears away from the voice that lies, and toward the Voice that never lies. Nouwen writes, "From all eternity, from long before you were born and became a part of history, you existed in God's heart. Long before your parents admired you or your friends acknowledged your gifts or your teachers, colleagues, and employers encouraged you, you were already 'chosen.' The eyes of love had seen you as precious, as of infinite beauty, as of eternal value."[7]

The eyes of Love *delight* in who you are. They find you beautiful in every way. They see *infinite beauty* in you. If this possibility seems foreign to you, I get it. I do. And that's why it's so important to sit with the truth of who God says you are.

He says you're beautiful . . . in every way.

---

7. Nouwen, *Life of the Beloved*, 53.

QUESTIONS TO ASK YOURSELF

Have you ever struggled to believe them when friends and others have spoken kind things about you?

Can you hear God affirming that you are beautiful in every way?

Do you believe that you are delighted in?

SCRIPTURE

"YOU ARE PRECIOUS
AND HONORED IN MY SIGHT,
AND . . . I LOVE YOU."

—ISAIAH 43:4

PRAYER

Father, I worship and praise You. You are beautiful. Today I ask that You would continue to open the eyes and ears of my heart to see You and hear You clearly. I choose to own the reality that I am Your beloved! Daily, I am given endless choices to believe You or to believe the lies that are swirling around me. So I commit to choosing what is true. I commit to choosing You. Speak to me through prayer, through Scripture, or through others. Speak, Lord, for Your servant is listening. Show me Your face, the face of Love that delights in who You made me to be.

AMEN.

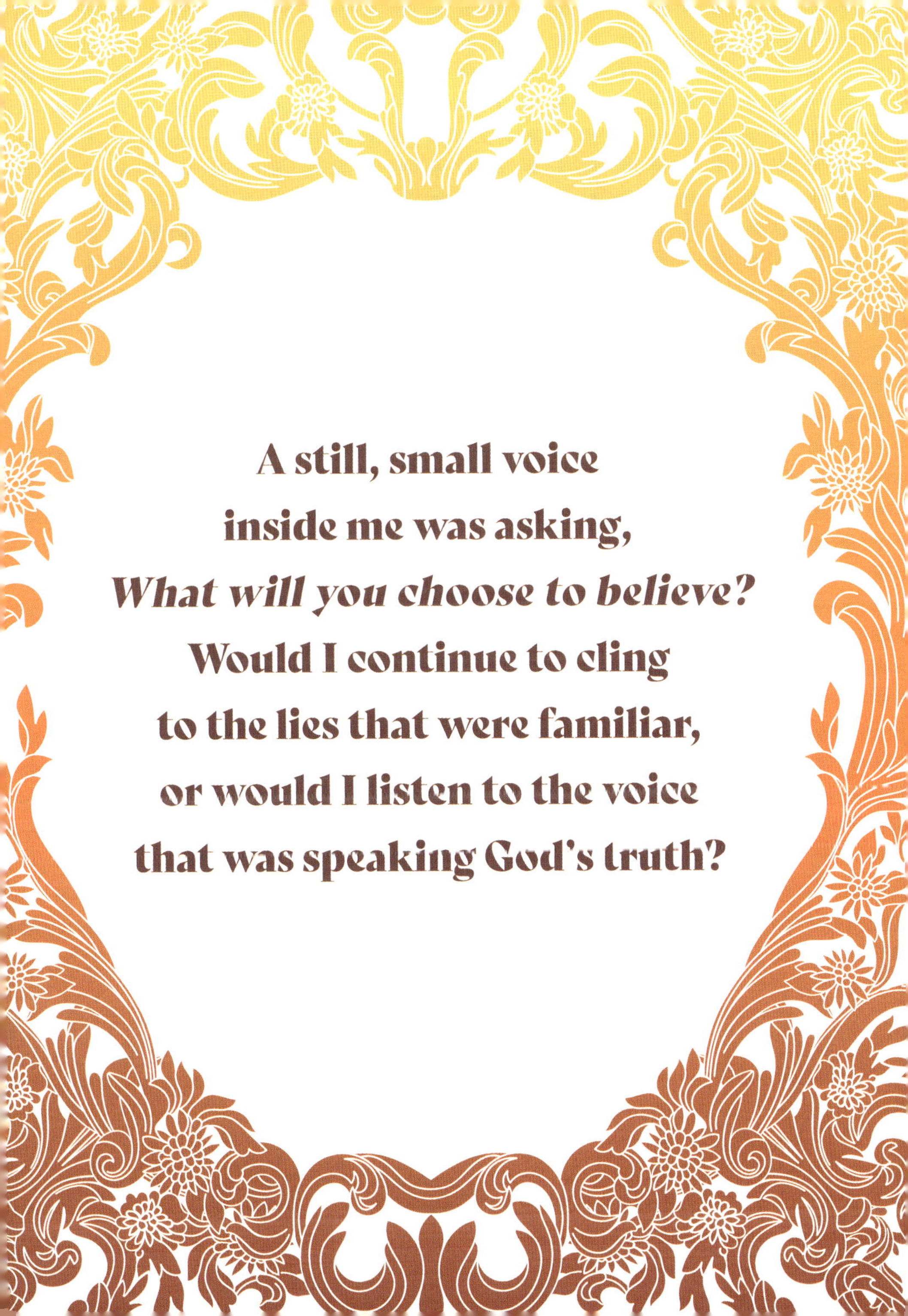

A still, small voice
inside me was asking,
What will you choose to believe?
Would I continue to cling
to the lies that were familiar,
or would I listen to the voice
that was speaking God's truth?

My love
for you
is
fierce...

Belovedness

SARAH KROGER

1:03 3:42

LIKE A MAMA BEAR

If you come across a bear in the woods, do you know what to do?

If not, this is your lucky day.

If you come across a bear, you're supposed to act big. And loud. You can stand on your toes and spread your arms to the sky, growling and acting mean. The experts say that a bear is feeling fear just like you are and usually they'll be happy enough to dodge you and go in a different direction.

But if you see a mama bear with her cubs? Throw that advice out the window.

What matters more to a mama bear than the fear she might feel when she sees you is the safety of her cubs. You do not want to threaten her babies. Because if you pose a threat to those young cubs, their mama is going to fight you. So, if you stumble upon a bear family, leave. If that's impossible, wait calmly and quietly until all the bears move away. Never, ever approach a mother bear with her cubs. Don't go near those babies. Don't look at them. Don't even think about them.

The love and protectiveness of a mama bear for her cubs is a *fierce* love. She will do anything to protect them.

You know what? In the family of God, *you are the cub*. You're the beloved. You're the one the Father will go to any length to protect.

The job of a parent—both bear parents and human parents—is twofold: to protect and to nurture. Parents are supposed to protect their young at any cost, and they are supposed to nurture their babies, physically and emotionally, by meeting their needs.

Here's the rub: none of us was raised by perfect human parents. That means that every one of us has needs—for safety, for care—that weren't met. I'm not saying that to throw any parents under the bus. But I am saying that to name the reality that every one of us has a deep heart-need for a parent who does not fail.

Maybe we were not protected physically when we were young. Maybe we weren't protected emotionally. Or it may be that we didn't receive the nurturing we needed. Perhaps one of our parents wasn't equipped to care for us in the ways we needed. And our hearts are hungry for that fierce love we were made for. We're hungry to have our needs met by the One whose love does not fail.

The prophet Hosea described God as that fierce mama bear. And the author of Deuteronomy described God as a mother eagle, saying that He is "like an eagle that stirs up its nest and hovers over its young, that spreads its wings to catch them and carries them aloft" (Deuteronomy 32:11). When a mother eagle stirs up the nest, she's making the nest less comfortable for her young. She's teaching them how to fly. She pushes the chicks toward the edge, and when they fall out, the mother eagle dips down and rescues her little ones, depositing them back in the nest one by one. It might seem like a crazy practice, but the mama bird knows her babies can't learn how to fly without falling. And as they get over their fear of falling, since they've experienced what it feels like, they'll work up the courage to spread their wings, leave the nest behind, and fly.

The mother eagle's love is fierce; she does not let her chick fall.

The mother bear's love is fierce; she puts herself on the line to protect her cub from harm.

If you didn't experience perfect protection or unfailing support from your parents, turn your face toward the Father whose love for you is fierce. Spend time with the One whose love does not fail.

QUESTIONS TO ASK YOURSELF

Can you imagine God as your fierce mama bear protector?

When have you experienced God's fierce love for you?

How have you felt God's protection of you?

SCRIPTURE

[THE LORD IS] LIKE AN EAGLE
THAT STIRS UP ITS NEST AND
HOVERS OVER ITS YOUNG,
THAT SPREADS ITS WINGS
TO CATCH THEM AND
CARRIES THEM ALOFT.

—DEUTERONOMY 32:11

PRAYER

God, You are strong, not weak. You are present, not neglectful. You are fierce. Father, You know me through and through. You know the ways that I have been loved well, and You know the ways that human love has failed me. You know the hurts that I continue to harbor in my heart. Lord, I offer them to You, and I turn to You as the only One who can love me perfectly.

AMEN.

If you didn't experience
perfect protection
or unfailing support
from your parents,
turn your face toward
the Father whose love
for you is fierce.

. . . and unending . . .

Belovedness

SARAH KROGER

1:06 3:42

NOT EVEN DEATH

When my husband and I got married, one of the most unexpectedly moving parts of the day was having everyone we loved together in the *same room*. They had all gathered to celebrate us and to send us off into the new season we were beginning. When I looked around that room and considered the sacrifice so many had made to be there, I felt overwhelmed. I've never experienced that magnitude of love concentrated in one place, and I never wanted it to end.

In our wiring as people, we were made to be loved. We were created to enjoy rich mutual friendships that enrich us and bless the world. We were designed to share life with a special someone, or a community of someones, who love us and have our backs.

But because of sin, we don't always experience the love God intends for us to receive. Maybe a relationship with a friend was ruptured, and now all that remains is an icy distance. Or perhaps the closeness we once had with a sibling has become strained. Maybe we've lost a parent to death or to divorce. Or perhaps the person whom we trusted most in the world betrayed us. The relationships that are most important to us can fracture or end in ways we'd never choose.

We were made for better things.

The truth is, we shouldn't hold the people in our lives to a standard they can't possibly meet. We may long for parents to love us with a perfect love. We may hunger for a spouse to love us perfectly. But they're all human, like us. No human is able to meet our hearts' deepest need for an unconditional love that does not fail.

Now for the good news: there is One who can.

We were made to experience unending love, and God's steadfast promise to us is that we *can* receive that perfect love in *Him*.

God's love for us—right now, in this moment—is real. It's sturdy. It's what is holding us together. God's love for us is available when we get fired from a job. Or as we wrestle with an addiction. Or when we receive a bad diagnosis. We can even access God's love for us as we return to the moments from childhood when we believed we were entirely alone and unprotected. We can receive God's perfect love.

I once heard a preacher talking about the virtues of faith, hope, and love. As the apostle Paul told the Corinthians in his first letter to them, "the greatest of these is love" (I Corinthians 13:13). The preacher pointed out that love persists for all eternity. "In heaven, we probably won't need faith. We will be completely united to God. We won't need hope, either. All the longings of our hearts will already be fulfilled in His presence. But love . . . love will abound. Perhaps," the preacher concluded, "that is why the greatest virtue is love. It lasts forever."

Let that sink in: *Love does not end.*

Saint Paul was convinced that nothing in this world can separate us from God's love for us in Jesus Christ. Nothing. Not even death (Romans 8:38).

Remember all those people at my wedding reception? While each one of those relationships, at some point, will end, the love we shared is not a waste of time—because any true love we experience on earth is a reflection of the powerful love of God. And that love is not bound by time. It continues! It's unending, because God *is* love (I John 4:16). So when we do experience love in our lives—the unbridled hugs from a nephew or niece, a tender word from a spouse, the fierce support of a friend who has our back—we're experiencing a taste of eternity.

QUESTIONS TO ASK YOURSELF

Who is someone who has loved you well, showing you what God's love is like?

Are you convinced that, like Paul says to us in Romans, nothing can separate us from the love of God? Why or why not?

SCRIPTURE

FOR I AM CONVINCED
THAT NEITHER DEATH NOR LIFE,
NEITHER ANGELS NOR DEMONS,
NEITHER THE PRESENT NOR THE FUTURE,
NOR ANY POWERS,
NEITHER HEIGHT NOR DEPTH,
NOR ANYTHING ELSE IN ALL CREATION,
WILL BE ABLE TO SEPARATE US
FROM THE LOVE OF GOD THAT IS
IN CHRIST JESUS OUR LORD.

—ROMANS 8:38–39

PRAYER

Lord, You are the Author of love. You are love itself. Thank You for all the moments I've had on this earth that are a foretaste of Your unending love. Thank You for each person in my life who has modeled Your steadfast love to me. Help me to know that there is nothing that can separate me from Your love. God, fill me with Your Spirit. Empower me to reflect Your unfailing love to those around me this day.

AMEN.

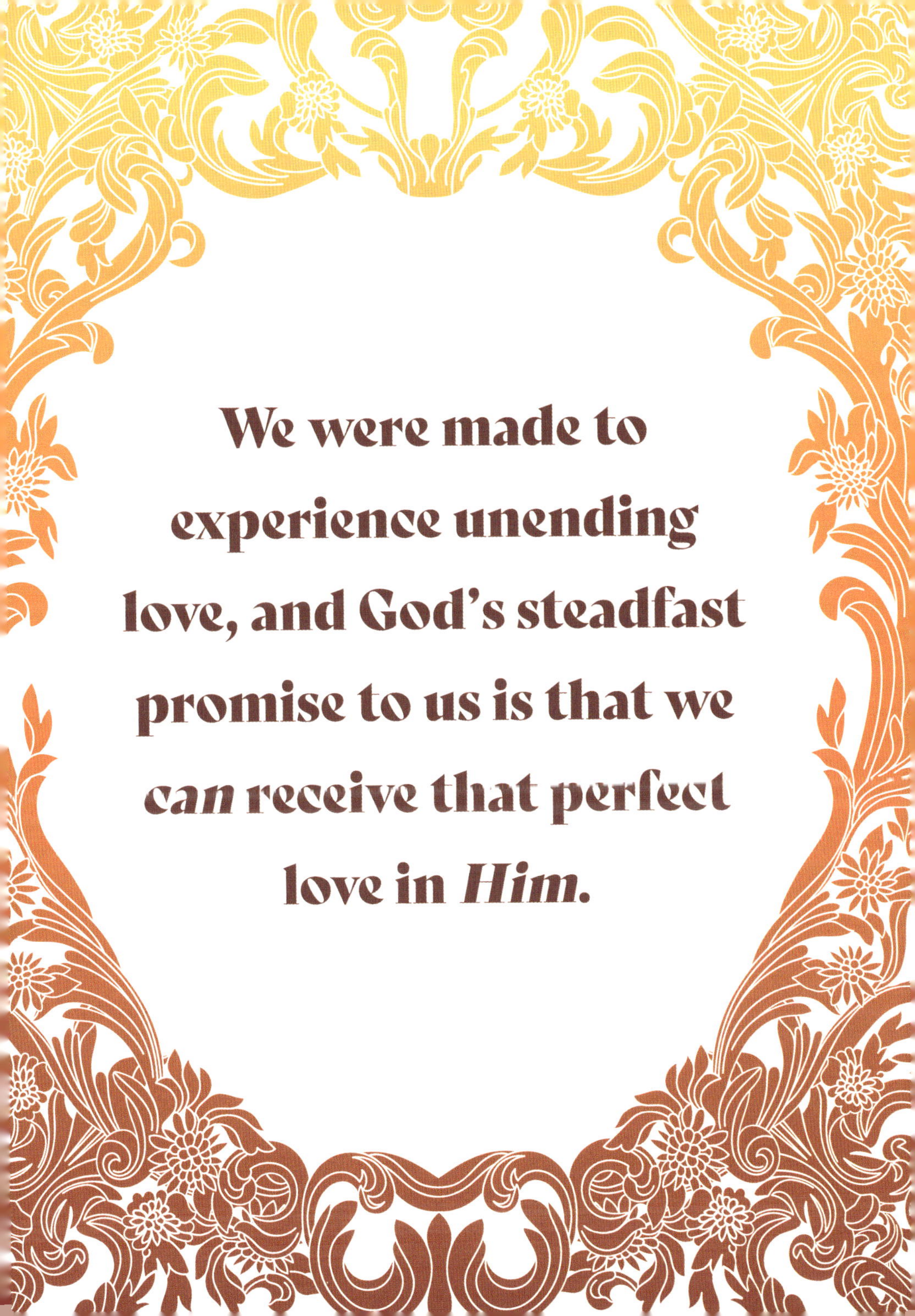
We were made to
experience unending
love, and God's steadfast
promise to us is that we
can receive that perfect
love in *Him*.

Any true love we experience on earth is a reflection of the powerful love of God.

-SARAH KROGER

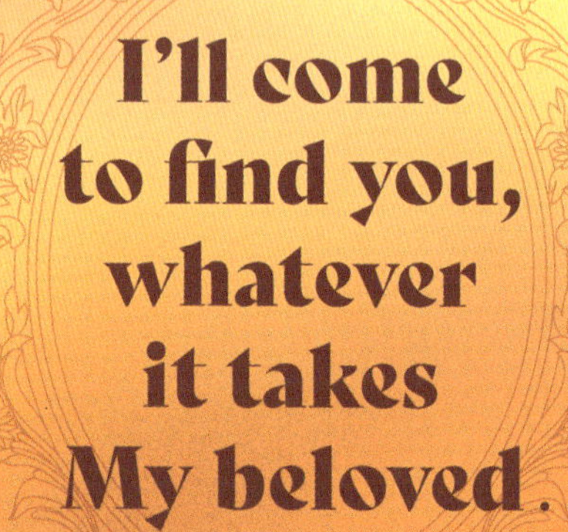

Belovedness

SARAH KROGER

1:08 3:42

HE LEAVES THE NINETY-NINE

Jesus, outlined in black, standing against a pale-blue sky, is holding a vulnerable little lamb in His arms, close to His chest.

It's the scene in a stained-glass window in a chapel that is dear to my heart. The chapel is located at a camp called Covecrest I attended as a teen. I later served as a counselor there during my college years, and I have returned to lead worship many times since. So, throughout various chapters of my life, that image has served as a kind of backdrop, a constant. It represents the Lord's consistent, faithful presence in every season of my life.

But if you know what the Bible says about the good Shepherd, the picture means even more. Both the Old and New Testaments of the Bible point to God as a Shepherd who is good. In Psalm 23, we pray with the psalmist, "The Lord is my shepherd" (Psalm 23:1). And then, when Jesus arrives on the scene, He announces, "I am the good shepherd" (John 10:11). Context is everything, and in Jesus's day, this was actually a bold thing to say. Jesus's first audience, who were Jews, would have known something about the character of the Shepherd who's revealed and revered in Psalm 23. The daily life of these folks was agrarian—it revolved around plants and weeds, birds and sheep. So they understood, intimately, what He was saying. He's a Provider. He's a Guide. He's a Comforter. He's a Protector. More than anything, He is *good.*

One day when Jesus was speaking to a group of tax collectors and reputable "sinners," the religious leaders were bothered that He was keeping company with such a rough crowd. So, wanting everyone to know what His Father's heart was like, Jesus told a story.

He asked His audience to imagine what it would be like to have a hundred sheep and to lose one. He invited them to imagine the shepherd searching far and wide until he found that one lost sheep. Then the shepherd joyfully would throw the sheep on his shoulders and walk home. There, he would welcome his neighbors and friends to rejoice with him (Luke 15:1–7). Jesus was describing the way His Father loves the one who has wandered off. The one who cheats on their test. The one who cheats on their taxes. The one who cheats on their spouse. Regardless of how far someone has wandered, no one is outside the reach of God.

Beloved, do you realize this is the Father's heart for you? When you feel lost, when you wander away, when you choose the idols of the world . . . He seeks you out and carries you on His shoulders. He rejoices in bringing you back into the fold. Notice, the trip back is not a "walk of shame." It's a celebration. This is the heart of the Father: *I'll come to find you, whatever it takes.*

That "finding" happened for me, as a teen, at Covecrest. Although I'd been raised in the Church, I clearly experienced what I call a "deeper conversion." I developed a deeper understanding of who Jesus was in my life. It wasn't a one-and-done conversion. It never is. Because we are distractible and sinful sheep who wander off again and again, Jesus's pursuit of us is *constant*. He's always coming to find us, and we are continually being converted. There are always more levels to uncover of His great love for us.

There have been times in my recent adult life when I've felt like I'm completely in the dark spiritually. I've felt like that one who's lost. I've felt like the sheep who wandered away from the Shepherd. But I've also felt Him reaching out for my hand in the darkness. He seeks me out and finds me. And every time He brings me back into the fold, I experience the colors and depths and wonders of His love in new ways.

He does the same for you. Wherever you are—from the highest mountain to the deepest valley—He pursues you, desiring to scoop you up and cradle you in His loving arms.

QUESTIONS TO ASK YOURSELF

Do you feel lost or found right now?

When has Jesus come to find you?

Do you believe that God will do whatever it takes to bring you home, again and again?

SCRIPTURE

"WHAT DO YOU THINK? IF A MAN OWNS A HUNDRED SHEEP, AND ONE OF THEM WANDERS AWAY, WILL HE NOT LEAVE THE NINETY-NINE ON THE HILLS AND GO TO LOOK FOR THE ONE THAT WANDERED OFF? AND IF HE FINDS IT, TRULY I TELL YOU, HE IS HAPPIER ABOUT THAT ONE SHEEP THAN ABOUT THE NINETY-NINE THAT DID NOT WANDER OFF. IN THE SAME WAY YOUR FATHER IN HEAVEN IS NOT WILLING THAT ANY OF THESE LITTLE ONES SHOULD PERISH."

—MATTHEW 18:12–14

PRAYER

Good Shepherd, I thank You that I belong to You. I believe that You provide. You guide. You comfort. You protect. I believe that You are good. And while I'd love to believe that I'm always a part of the ninety-nine, a reliable sheep who never strays, You know my heart. You know the ways in which I am tempted to wander after things that do not satisfy me. You know how I seek security and comfort in that which is not You. Forgive me. Sweep me up in Your arms and hold me close to Your heart. Today, I choose to embrace my belovedness. Thank You for Your love that does not fail.

AMEN.

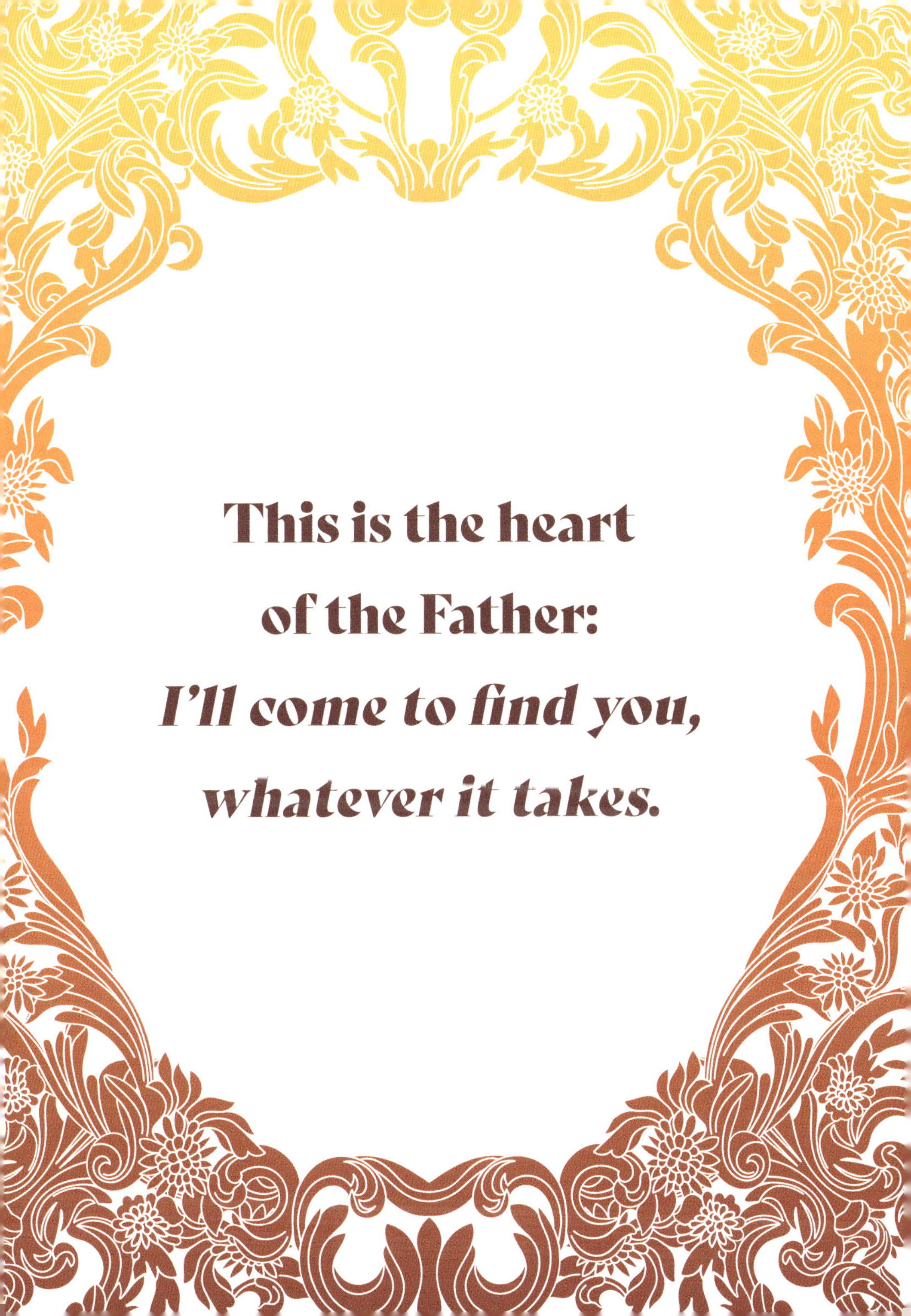
This is the heart
of the Father:
*I'll come to find you,
whatever it takes.*

You've owned the mess you see in the mirror . . .

Belovedness

SARAH KROGER

1:18 3:42

MESS IN THE MIRROR

Why can't you seem to form coherent sentences? They're going to figure out you're an imposter.

What is wrong with you?!

These words, words I wouldn't dream of saying to anyone else, were just a part the junk I was hurling at myself.

I had done an interview with a podcast host, and for some reason, I just couldn't get in the flow. A few days later, I had a tough phone call that didn't unfold the way I'd hoped it would. To top it all off, I was comparing myself to other artists on social media who communicated so well. I wasn't showing up in the world the way I wanted to and knew I could. Though so much of what went wrong during the week was out of my control, I blamed myself for it all.

What do *you* see when you look in the mirror? I don't mean the zit or the bad haircut or whatever physical features you may not like. What do you see when you look at the person within? Many of us are quick to own the negative things we believe about ourselves. Oddly, we worry that the positive things about us are actually "too good to be true." And we accept the negative things as "just the way we are."

I confess there are times when I look in the mirror and don't have the vision to see what God saw when He made me. I'm not seeing the person God designed me to be. Rather than seeing what I am, I only see what I'm *not.* I get frustrated with the things I struggled with last year, and am struggling with today, and may still be struggling with six months from now.

I'm frustrated that I'm not perfect.

I see the patterns that I want to change but haven't been able to break.

I find myself struggling with the same . . . old . . . stuff. And left to my own devices, allowing the accusing voice unfettered access to my mind, I'd be consumed.

But the author of Lamentations says, "Because of the LORD's great love we are not consumed" (Lamentations 3:22). *Amen?* I do not have to be consumed by the voices in my head.

When I get stuck in this way, God often reminds me, *Perfection isn't possible for you. Just Me.* Or, *You'll never have all the answers, but I do.* And I know it sounds odd, but it's almost like my brain doesn't realize that until God reminds me. Because my brain insists that perfection is possible, and thus I'm at war within myself.

When I remind myself of the truth, I'm able to steady myself on solid ground again. I'm reminded that all the big feelings inside me are just that: *feelings*. When they're coming at me, one after another, it can be intense. They're *valid*. They have a purpose: They alert me to what's going on internally. Feelings aren't inherently bad, but they don't always tell me the full truth.

The truth is that I'm a human who's trying my best and makes mistakes.

The truth is that I am made in His image.

The truth is that I am beloved.

The truth is that tomorrow is a new day, and God's Word assures me that His mercies are new every morning (Lamentations 3:23). If His mercies for me are new every morning, then my mercies for myself can also be new every morning. My mercies for *others* can be new every morning too. This is who God is and what He does.

So, when I look in the mirror and a voice hisses lies about who I am, or who God is, I can choose to tell myself the truth. I can receive the goodness of God's fresh mercy, for me and for others, and tell myself what is true.

I'm human.

I'm good.

I'm beloved.

You are too.

QUESTIONS TO ASK YOURSELF

What do you see on social media that drags you into the comparison game?

In what area of your life do you want to be *perfect*?

How can you make space to listen to the Voice of truth today? What is He saying to you?

SCRIPTURE

BECAUSE OF
THE LORD'S GREAT LOVE
WE ARE NOT CONSUMED,
FOR HIS COMPASSIONS NEVER FAIL.
THEY ARE NEW EVERY MORNING;
GREAT IS YOUR FAITHFULNESS.

—LAMENTATIONS 3:22–23

PRAYER

Faithful God, You are a good Creator. When You created the world, day by day, You looked at what You made and announced, "It is good." God, I am choosing to believe that I am good because You made me. All of Your works are wonderful. I confess there are times when I look in the mirror and my vision is blurry. It fails me. I don't see what You see. Father, renew me. Give me Your vision. Help me to embrace what is most true. I place myself in Your loving hands.

AMEN.

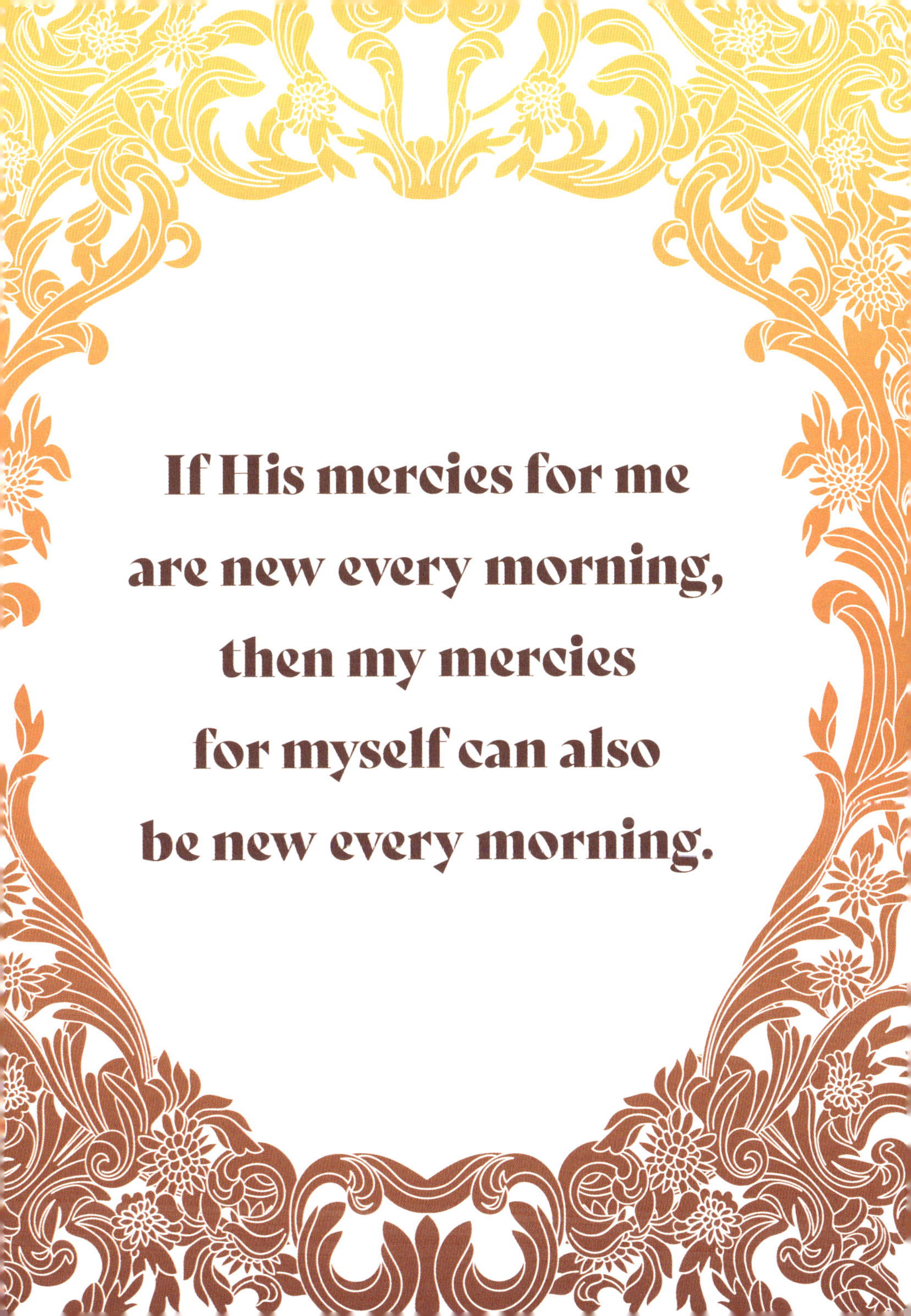
If His mercies for me
are new every morning,
then my mercies
for myself can also
be new every morning.

You've owned the lies that you're just not enough...

Belovedness

SARAH KROGER

1:23

3:42

BEING WOUNDABLE

I was seven years old, working on a project for school. I had to make a banner for religion class, and my dad was helping me.

At one point, he looked at it and said, "It's not right. You're doing it wrong. Just let me do it."

So I watched as my dad took over and made it absolutely perfect. (I didn't tell my teacher, but it was obvious to everyone that no seven-year-old had made that banner.)

Even though I'm sure my dad didn't intend to hurt me, I remember feeling totally dejected. The project was designed for me to express myself, and my self-expression had been deemed to be not good enough. A few years ago, I realized that *on that day* a seed was planted in me. But instead of a beautiful flower, a weed started to grow. It made me feel like my contribution was unworthy. It made me question my creativity. If what I made wasn't perfect, I should keep it to myself. That tiny little seed took root, and it manifested in all kinds of ugly ways.

C. S. Lewis said that "to love at all is to be vulnerable." The word *vulnerable*, literally translated, means "woundable." In my vulnerability, I'd been wounded by one of the people I trusted most. And I suspect that you have, as well. Maybe you can pinpoint a moment in time when the seed of a weed was planted. But it might also be true that you can't point to a moment. And yet the seed was planted—in an instant or over many years—during a time when you were at your most vulnerable. If harm befell you, maybe you started to believe that it was what you deserved. If a parent left, maybe you believed you weren't worth sticking around for. And before you know it, the lie takes root and starts wreaking havoc.

A weed in the garden steals nutrients and water from the plants around it. Because weeds tend to grow faster, they can tower over the plants and flowers you're actually trying to grow, keeping them from getting sunlight. If that isn't frustrating enough, some weeds actually give off certain chemicals in the soil that stunt the growth of the plants nearby.

You know how when you pull up a weed by the roots, it can have those chunks of dirt attached? When you see how extensively those roots have spread out, you realize how many resources it's been stealing from the good and beautiful things you are hoping to grow.

The work God invites us to do includes unearthing the lies that have seeped into the soil of our lives and taken root. Even though His Spirit can open our eyes to these weeds, it's our job to uproot them.

The way we uproot them starts by tuning our ears to the Voice that speaks truth. We *uproot* falsehood by *steeping ourselves* in truth. Nouwen states, "Every time you listen with great attentiveness to the voice that calls you the Beloved, you will discover within yourself a desire to hear that voice longer and more deeply."[8]

As truth resounds in your spirit, the weeds get weaker and easier to pull out.

Precious friend, for years you have owned the lies from your past. And now, in this moment, God is inviting you to listen to His voice, the one that calls you Beloved.

---

8. Nouwen, *Life of the Beloved*, 37.

QUESTIONS TO ASK YOURSELF

What seed of a weed was planted in you when you were young?

What weeds need to be uprooted in the garden of your heart?

What is God saying to you today? Spend time listening in the silence.

SCRIPTURE

"AND YOU WILL
KNOW THE TRUTH,
AND THE TRUTH
WILL SET YOU FREE."

—JOHN 8:32 ESV

PRAYER

God, I turn my heart toward You. When Your Son came to earth, He announced that He is Truth. The enemy is a liar and a deceiver; there is no truth in him. He is the father of lies. So I turn to You as the Father of truth, the Source of all that is good. You know what lies I have internalized. Expose and uproot them all. I don't want them taking up space in the garden of my heart. Take them from me and replace them with what is most true. Do what only You can do in me so that I can live in the freedom of Your love.

AMEN.

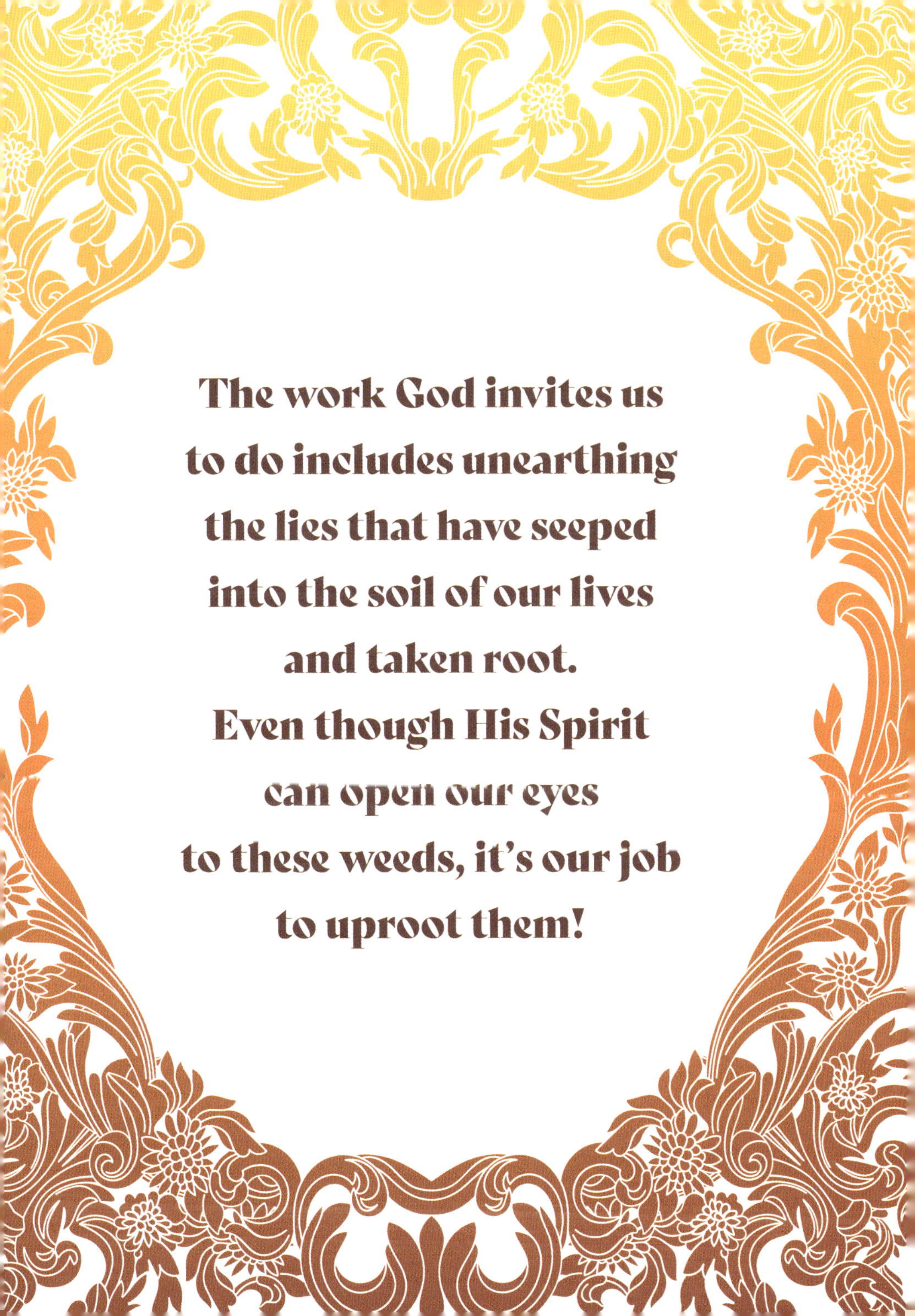
The work God invites us
to do includes unearthing
the lies that have seeped
into the soil of our lives
and taken root.
Even though His Spirit
can open our eyes
to these weeds, it's our job
to uproot them!

You've been so blinded by all your comparing. It's time to own your belovedness . . .

Belovedness

SARAH KROGER

1:27 3:42

BE *YOU*

President Theodore Roosevelt once noted, "Comparison is the thief of joy."

There's no winning at the comparison game. Truly, it might be the *worst* game ever. When we compare ourselves to others, we're going to feel either superior or inferior, and neither of those is helpful.

Trust me, I've gotten tangled up in that awful game plenty of times.

There was a season when I was constantly comparing myself with others. For me, it wasn't about brains or beauty or bank accounts. I was comparing myself with other Christian artists. I'll be honest, it's more than a little embarrassing to admit.

I wanted their talent.

I wanted his confidence.

I wanted her voice.

The lie I'd believed was that in order to do what God had called me to do, I had to be someone *other* than who God made *me* to be. If you read that sentence carefully, you can spot just how silly of a notion it really is. Left to my own thoughts, I believed that I was not enough, that I would never be enough. This prevented me from dreaming and doing. Regardless of my goal, I was convinced that I'd never make it.

Wherever you are in your journey today, you have likely experienced something similar. You might suspect that if you were better in one area, or more disciplined in another, you'd be enough. Enough for yourself. Enough for others. Enough for God. Or you might believe that you're deficient because you don't have the spiritual gift that God gave to someone you admire and respect. You might believe the lie that you need to be someone *other* than exactly who God has made you to be.

Even though it was easy for me to get distracted by the lies, I listened for the gentle Voice of the Lord weaving a different narrative in my heart:

Sarah, I gave you your mind.

Sarah, I gave you your heart.

Sarah, I gave you your voice.

Sarah, I have written a story in your life that is yours alone. No one else can share what I've given to you.

Sarah, there are children of Mine who need to receive exactly what you have to share.

Sarah, you are exactly as I made you to be.

Beloved, I want you to listen to the One who made you exactly as you are. As C. S. Lewis said, "Be weird. Be random. Be who you are. Because you never know who would love the person you hide."

No one else can offer the world what you can offer. You are an entirely unique and unrepeatable combination of gifts, quirks, passions, scars, and skills. Between the way God knit you together in the beginning and the unique set of experiences you've had, no one else on the planet—past, present, or future—can impact the world the specific way that you can.

Say *no* to the comparison game. *Do not play.* Comparison can steal your joy and rob the world of your unique offering. Beloved, say *yes* to being exactly who God made you to be.

QUESTIONS TO ASK YOURSELF

When you play the comparison game, are you more tempted by thoughts of superiority or inferiority?

What is the area, today, in which you feel like you're not enough?

When you ask God to show you the gift(s) that *only you* can offer the world, what is it?

SCRIPTURE

EACH ONE SHOULD
TEST THEIR OWN ACTIONS.
THEN THEY CAN TAKE PRIDE
IN THEMSELVES ALONE,
WITHOUT COMPARING THEMSELVES
TO SOMEONE ELSE.

—GALATIANS 6:4

PRAYER

Father, I thank You for making me exactly as I am. Open my eyes to the gifts You have placed in me, especially the ones I may be blind to. I confess that I'm tempted to compare myself to others, Lord. Forgive me. Help me resist. I commit to recognize and honor what is unique and special about others, and I commit to do the same for myself. May You be glorified in me, as my Maker, as I strive to use the gifts You have placed inside me. Help me to delight in who You have made me to be.

AMEN.

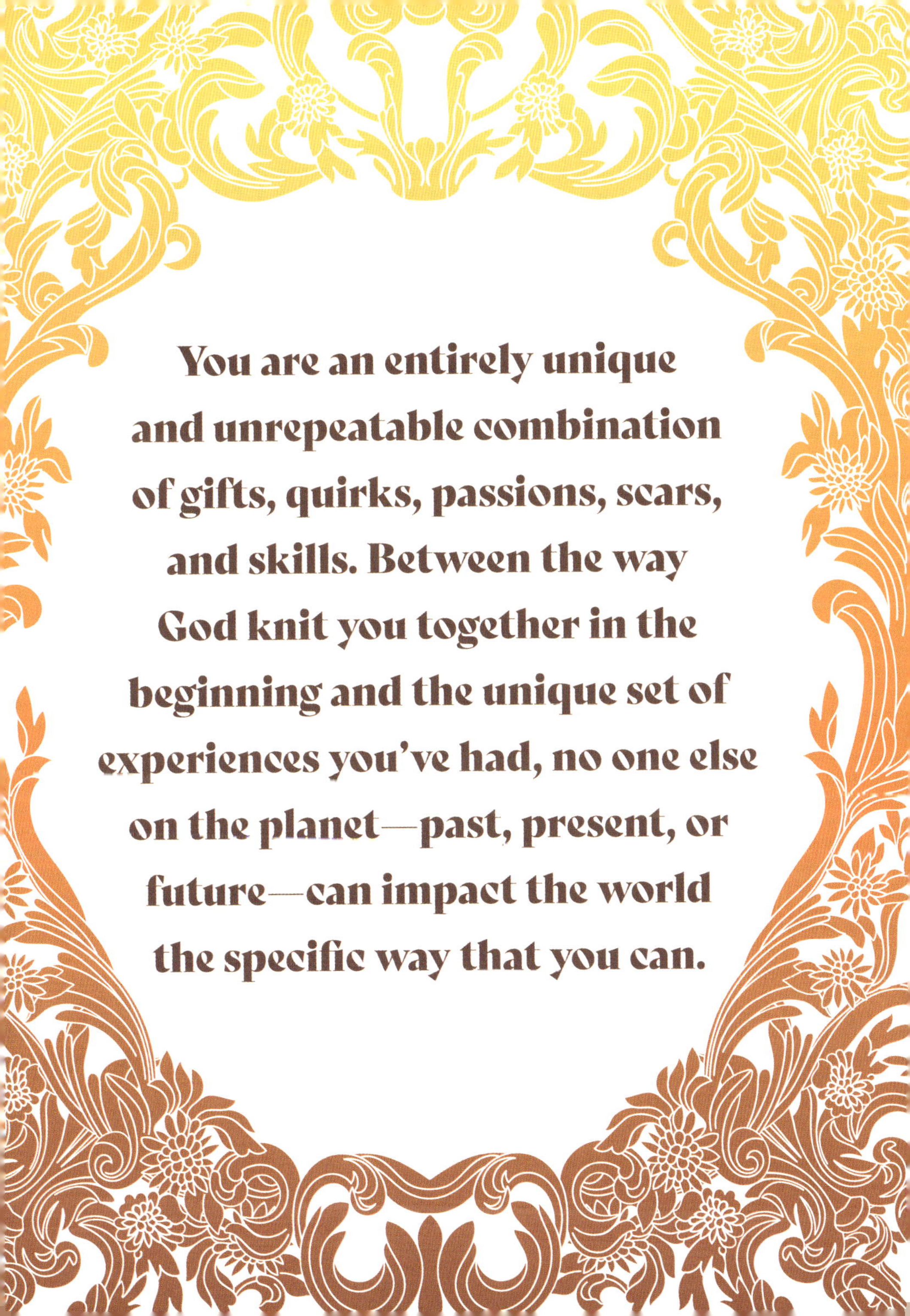
You are an entirely unique
and unrepeatable combination
of gifts, quirks, passions, scars,
and skills. Between the way
God knit you together in the
beginning and the unique set of
experiences you've had, no one else
on the planet—past, present, or
future—can impact the world
the specific way that you can.

Belovedness

SARAH KROGER

2:14 3:42

GOD'S GLORY IN YOU

Have you ever laid eyes on a squishy little infant who just melts your heart? Maybe you were the parent of said infant. Maybe you were the favorite uncle or auntie. Or maybe you were just strolling along the sidewalk and caught a glimpse of a fresh-out-of-the-oven little human. There is just so much to *love* about these squirmy little creatures. It's easy to love them *completely*.

But as I mentioned earlier, none of us will be loved perfectly by other human beings. And that's why we *need* to receive God's perfect love.

What I want you to hear is that God loves you completely. Perfectly. Steadfastly. Without fail. His love isn't fragile or fleeting. That said, you have to open yourself up to receive that love.

One of the gifts God has given me to help me receive His love is the gift of therapy. In my own personal therapy journey, I've had to really work on learning how to love myself. This can often get confused with "self-care." But I'm not talking about baths or candles or oils or bubbles here (although I do love all those things). I'm talking about true self-love that comes from God. Did you know that

God wants us to love ourselves?

When a smarty-pants theological know-it-all approached Jesus, he asked Him what the most important commandment was. "Easy," Jesus said (paraphrasing here). "Love God." And then He added, "The second is this: 'Love your neighbor as yourself.'"

Those are our marching orders.

Those of us who grew up in church have heard the Big Two countless times: love God; love people. But did you notice that Jesus is really specific about how we're supposed to love other people? We're supposed to love *other people* the way that we love *ourselves*. And what that means is that Jesus *assumes* that we love ourselves. He's not throwing shade; He's honoring the fact that we *ought* to love ourselves! And we do, right? If we're hungry, we grab something from the fridge. If we're tired, we fall into bed and go to sleep. If we have nothing to wear to school or to work, we go to the mall or we order what we need from Amazon. Jesus *assumes* that we know how to love ourselves. He assumes it because it's how we're wired.

We *should* love ourselves. But we're not always so good at it, are we?

Because we are completely loved by God, I want to name the value of learning to love ourselves the way that God loves us. That's some of the work I've done in therapy. Because despite knowing in our heads that God loves us, it can take some work to receive all of that love in our very beings. When we commit to loving ourselves the way that God loves us—*completely*—we discover the goodness that He sees in us. And we own the life-giving reality that we don't have to be anyone other than who we are. We affirm that the world needs us as we are because there's a piece of God's glory in each of us that only we can shine, only we can reflect to the world.

Did you know that?

As I did the therapeutic work to learn to love myself the way that God does, completely, I began to realize there is a piece of goodness and love and beauty in me that only I can give to the world. And the same is true for you. There is goodness and love and beauty in you that only you can give to the world. God put it in you, and learning to accept that is a huge part of the life of discipleship.

Because God loves you completely, do the work to love yourself completely.

QUESTIONS TO ASK YOURSELF

How easy or difficult is it for you to believe that God loves you, entirely?

What are some of the ways that you care for your body, your mind, and your heart on a daily basis? Are there ways you could be showing up for yourself even more?

What kind of "work" have you done to better love yourself the way God loves you?

SCRIPTURE

ONE OF THE TEACHERS
OF THE LAW. . . ASKED [JESUS],
"OF ALL THE COMMANDMENTS,
WHICH IS THE MOST IMPORTANT?"

"THE MOST IMPORTANT ONE,"
ANSWERED JESUS, "IS THIS: 'HEAR, O ISRAEL:
THE LORD OUR GOD, THE LORD IS ONE.
LOVE THE LORD YOUR GOD WITH ALL YOUR
HEART AND WITH ALL YOUR SOUL AND
WITH ALL YOUR MIND AND WITH ALL YOUR
STRENGTH.' THE SECOND IS THIS: 'LOVE
YOUR NEIGHBOR AS YOURSELF.' THERE IS
NO COMMANDMENT GREATER THAN THESE."

—MARK 12:28–31

PRAYER

Gracious Father, I thank You for sculpting me with Your own hands and for bringing me into this world. When I think of the infant I once was, I can't help but receive Your unending love for me. I confess that I struggle to love myself with the wholehearted love You offer to me. Sometimes I only see my flaws. I relive my weakest moments. Forgive me. Lord, give me the courage to do the work of seeing myself as You see me: in therapy, in prayer, in Your Word, in community. Speak truth to my heart, Father, and help me receive it.

AMEN.

There is goodness
and love and beauty
in you that only you
can give to the world.

...and fully known...

Belovedness

SARAH KROGER

2:19 3:42

BEING FULLY KNOWN

I can't eat gluten.

I wish I could, but I can't.

There are moments when I'd *like* to eat gluten, but my body has told me it's not a good idea. It is what it is. Sometimes my husband is out at a café, meeting with a client, and he sees that they offer gluten-free options. He almost always brings something home for me. It might be a sweet blueberry muffin or a savory empanada. Honestly, it could be a cookie-shaped piece of cardboard, and I would love it. I'd love it because it reminds me that my husband *knows* me. He sees me. He knows what makes my face light up with joy. Honestly, gluten-free treats are my version of a dozen red roses. I feel known and loved when he brings me those beautiful, delicious carbs. Besides, you can't eat roses.

It's not just my husband either. Recently, some close friends hosted a dinner party, and they made sure to provide a gluten-free choice for me. These friends who know me and love me don't have to call ahead to ask if I have any dietary restrictions, because they *know*. They remember. They care. They accommodate.

They also know I'm wildly enraged by fire ants. They know I have a quirky sense of humor. And the fact that I am known by them makes me feel loved because we were made to be known *intimately.*

In *Life of the Beloved* Nouwen narrates the way that God knows us and loves us with this intimacy. He writes:

> *I look at you with infinite tenderness and care for you with a care more intimate than that of a mother for her child. I have counted every hair on your head and guided you at every step. Wherever you go, I go with you, and wherever you rest, I keep watch. I will give you food that will satisfy all your hunger and drink that will quench all your thirst. I will not hide my face from you. You know me as your own as I know you as my own.*[9]

When God chose Jeremiah to be His agent in the world, He announced, "Before I formed you in the womb I knew you, before you were born I set you apart" (Jeremiah 1:5). And while Jeremiah certainly had a special assignment, the same is true for each of us. Before you were conceived, God had thought of you. God knew you intimately. God lovingly knit you together exactly as you are, forming your shape with His own hands.

Beloved, you are completely loved and fully known.

---

9. Nouwen, *Life of the Beloved, 36–37.*

That thing you're allergic to? God knows.

The one person on the planet from any era whom you'd choose to sit across from and talk with for hours? God knows.

The thing that sets you off and makes you absolutely furious? God knows.

That thing you find hilarious even if no one else does? God knows.

Many people see us, but they don't know us. Some people know us, but they don't love us. God sees you and knows you intimately, and He loves you. Let that bring peace to your soul today.

QUESTIONS TO ASK YOURSELF

What makes you feel seen and known
by someone in your family?

What makes you feel seen and known
by one of your close friends?

What do you wish others knew about you?

SCRIPTURE

MY FRAME WAS NOT HIDDEN
FROM YOU WHEN I WAS MADE
IN THE SECRET PLACE,
WHEN I WAS WOVEN TOGETHER
IN THE DEPTHS OF THE EARTH.
YOUR EYES SAW MY UNFORMED BODY;
ALL THE DAYS ORDAINED FOR ME
WERE WRITTEN IN YOUR BOOK
BEFORE ONE OF THEM CAME TO BE.

—PSALM 139:15–16

PRAYER

Father and Creator, I belong to You. You formed me in my mother's womb, and You knew me before I was born. You know what brings me joy. You know what makes me furious. You know what burdens my heart. You know every single fear I carry. And when You see me, I believe that You look on me with tenderness and care. You know me inside and out, and still You love me. I am Yours, and You are mine. Lord, open my eyes to see what You see. Teach me how to love myself, and love others, with the generous love You offer.

AMEN.

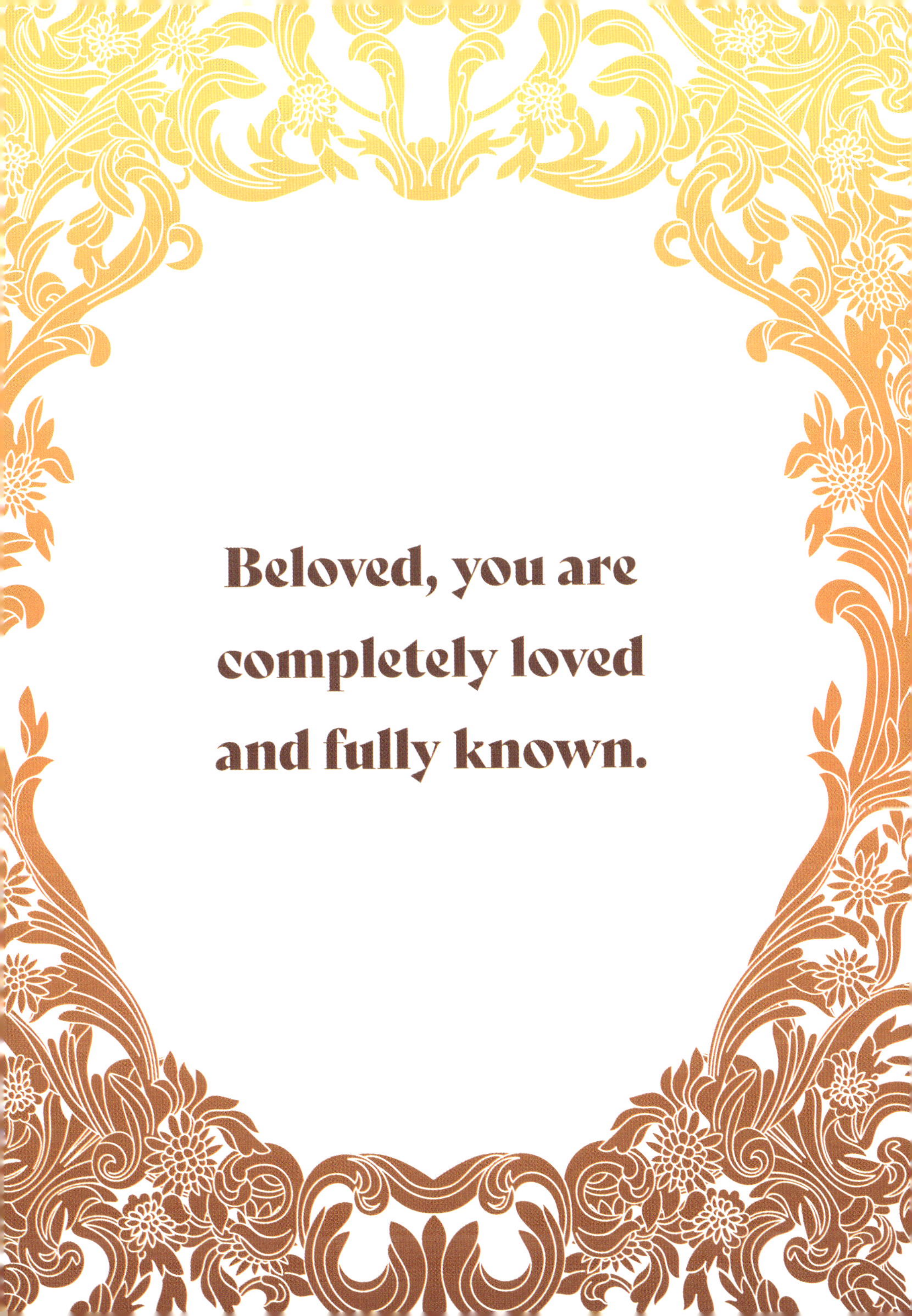

Beloved, you are completely loved and fully known.

Beloved,
believe
He died
to make
your heart
His home...

Belovedness

SARAH KROGER

2:23 3:42

ALIVE IN YOU

Have you ever heard someone say that Jesus lives inside of us?

It's weird, right? It's hard not to picture a little inch-high figurine dwelling inside your ribs where your heart is nestled. If it's a lot for us to wrap our minds around, it was even more so for Jesus's disciples.

At the end of His ministry, Jesus knew He was about to return to His Father, and He was preparing His disciples for this. He warned them that they would face opposition from those who had not known Him or His Father. Explaining to them, "I am going to Him who sent Me," He then assured them, "It is for your good that I am going away" (John 16:5–7 NIV).

And that just does not make any sense, does it? If you've lost someone you love, someone you wanted to be near, it doesn't seem "good."

Recognizing the disconnect on their faces, Jesus promised, "Unless I go away, the Advocate will not come to you; but if I go, I will send Him to you" (John 16:7).

If you've spent a minute in church, you might know that this

"Advocate" Jesus was talking about is the Holy Spirit. But His followers at the time? They had no clue what He meant.

What they couldn't know in that moment was that the Holy Spirit was coming. The Holy Spirit was going to dwell inside them—live in them!—as a companion. As a light. As a guide.

Jesus sent us the Spirit for our good. Jesus was fully divine, but also fully human. His time on earth in that physical, bodily form had to end eventually. But He also promised that He would never leave us. And thus His Spirit remains with us. When we allow the fire of His Spirit to burn within us, we are moved to action. We are purified. We can see the path before us illuminated. As we tune our ears to listen for God's Spirit, we can learn His voice.

Nouwen shares, of our inherent belovedness, "That's the truth spoken by the voice that says, 'You are my Beloved.' Listening to that voice with great inner attentiveness, I hear at my center words that say, 'I have called you by name, from the very beginning. You are mine and I am yours. You are my Beloved, on you my favor rests'."[10]

Are you able to hear that voice at your center? Are you able to hear God naming the truth of your belovedness? I learned this in an intimate way spending time with my spiritual director, who taught me that we *can* learn to hear God's voice. We can discern between

---

10. Nouwen, *Life of the Beloved*, 36.

the voice of the evil one and the voice of God. We can begin to recognize the inflection. The tone.

When you hear condemnation? That's the enemy. A message of hopelessness? That's the deceiver. Overly harsh? It's the voice that lies.

The good news is that because Jesus really does live *in us,* we are able to recognize His gentle voice speaking to our hearts. We can pick it out over all of the noise. And that means we can welcome and embrace what is most true.

QUESTIONS TO ASK YOURSELF

Do you have an awareness
of Jesus living in you?

How have you experienced
the comfort and guidance of the Holy Spirit?

Are you able to recognize,
and reject, the voice that lies?

SCRIPTURE

"BUT NOW I AM GOING TO HIM WHO SENT ME. NONE OF YOU ASKS ME, 'WHERE ARE YOU GOING?' RATHER, YOU ARE FILLED WITH GRIEF BECAUSE I HAVE SAID THESE THINGS. BUT VERY TRULY I TELL YOU, IT IS FOR YOUR GOOD THAT I AM GOING AWAY. UNLESS I GO AWAY, THE ADVOCATE WILL NOT COME TO YOU; BUT IF I GO, I WILL SEND HIM TO YOU."

—JOHN 16:5–7

PRAYER

Gracious and loving God, You are good. From the beginning, You have known me and loved me. You sent Your Son, Jesus, to die so that I could live. And You sent the gift of Your Holy Spirit so that I could experience Your palpable grace today. Thank You, God. Continue to make Your home in my heart. Live at the center of my being so that I can know Your closeness minute by minute. And give me the courage to walk in obedience to You. Thank You for the gift of Your presence in me, for the joy of Your closeness to me.

AMEN.

As we tune
our ears to listen
for God's Spirit,
we can learn
His voice.

It's time to own your belovedness

Belovedness

SARAH KROGER

3:18 3:42

ON YOU MY FAVOR RESTS

"You've changed."

That's what my manager, who's known me for years, said to me recently.

"Really," he continued. "There's something different about the way you show up in meetings. The way you carry yourself. The way you speak up."

It's true. I'm different these days. Part of it is my age. I simply don't care as much what people are thinking about me. I've realized they're actually not thinking about me as much as they're thinking about themselves and everything going on in their own lives. It's just how we are. Each of us is in our own little world.

I'm also enjoying the freedom that comes with owning my belovedness. And, like my manager, other people can tell. It shows up in how I walk into a room, whether it's a writing room, a friend's house, or a crowded room where I don't know anybody. It shows up in my relationships. It shows up in how I lead worship. I feel so much more free, so much happier with who God has made me to be.

In searching for words to explain the shift that's happened inside me, I'd choose the language Nouwen uses: "Though the experience of being the Beloved has never been completely absent from my life, I never claimed it as my core truth. I kept running around it in large or small circles, always looking for someone or something able to convince me of my Belovedness." *Gosh, he gets me.* Nouwen continues, "It was as if I kept refusing to hear the voice that speaks from the very depth of my being and says, 'You are my Beloved, on you my favor rests.'" Nouwen concludes, "That voice has always been there, but it seems that I was much more eager to listen to other, louder voices saying: 'Prove that you are worth something: do something relevant, spectacular, or powerful, and then you will earn the love you so desire.'"[11]

Does that human temptation resonate with you as well? Do you know what it's like to feel as if you have to prove that you're lovable?

For so many years, I felt like a stranger in my own body. I get emotional just thinking about it. There were years when I wanted to be someone else. And I believed that I *should be* someone else!

But today? Today I love how God made me. I'm not perfect, but I love myself. Nah, it's more than that. I *like* myself. Because that's another level, right? I like who God made me to be, which is such a gift.

I believe that everybody deserves to experience the type of

11. Nouwen, *Life of the Beloved*, 33–34.

radical self-acceptance that springs from knowing, in our deepest places, that we are God's beloved. God has not made a mistake in our unique design. There's an inherent dignity in owning our belovedness.

I like that I'm quirky.

I like that I laugh at stupid things.

I like using silly voices when I talk to my husband.

I like that I make up random jingles in my head.

I like this voice that God has given me, and how I get to use it.

I like the way I'm able to express myself through song.

I like the way my brain is wired.

And there absolutely was a day when I was mortified about every one of these things.

Friend, it's time to stop trying to earn your belovedness and start trying to own your belovedness. "Beloved" isn't a badge to earn, a club to join, or a gift to withhold from others. It's our identity. It's our name. And it's the strength we need for the journey. You are the beloved. Period. Full stop. There is nothing you've done, nothing that's been done to you, nothing that's been said to you, no lie you've believed, no mistake you've made, no sin you've committed, nothing that can take away your identity as a beloved child of God.

It's time to own it.

QUESTIONS TO ASK YOURSELF

Do you like yourself?

Are you open to allowing God to change you?

Have you tried to prove to others that you're worth loving? How?

SCRIPTURE

AND I PRAY THAT YOU,
BEING ROOTED AND ESTABLISHED
IN LOVE, MAY HAVE POWER,
TOGETHER WITH ALL THE LORD'S
HOLY PEOPLE, TO GRASP HOW
WIDE AND LONG AND HIGH AND
DEEP IS THE LOVE OF CHRIST,
AND TO KNOW THIS LOVE THAT
SURPASSES KNOWLEDGE—THAT YOU
MAY BE FILLED TO THE MEASURE
OF ALL THE FULLNESS OF GOD.

—EPHESIANS 3:17–19

PRAYER

God, You are mighty. You are holy. You are worthy of all our love and adoration. God, I recognize the ways in which I haven't readily received the gifts You've given me. I haven't owned my belovedness. I've resisted. I've refused. Forgive me. Help me see that there's nothing I can do to make You love me more. Help me hear Your gentle and kind voice assuring me, You are My Beloved; on you My favor rests. *Today I receive the fullness of Your love for me. Today I own my belovedness. Transform me into Your image so that I may love myself and others the way You do.*

AMEN.

"Beloved" isn't
a badge to earn,
a club to join, or
a gift to withhold
from others.
It's our identity.

You've owned your fear and all
your self-loathing
You've owned the voices inside of
your head
You've owned the shame and
reproach of your failure
It's time to own your belovedness

You've owned your past and how
it's defined you
You've owned everything
everybody else says
It's time to hear what your Father
has spoken
It's time to own your belovedness

He says, "You're mine, I smiled
when I made you
I find you beautiful in every way
My love for you is fierce and
unending
I'll come to find you, whatever it
takes
My beloved"

You've owned the mess you see in
the mirror
You've owned the lies that you're
just not enough
You've been so blinded by all you're
comparing
It's time to own your belovedness

He says, "You're mine, I smiled
when I made you
I find you beautiful in every way
My love for you is fierce and
unending
I'll come to find you, whatever it
takes
My beloved"

You are completely loved and fully
known
Beloved, believe He died to make
your heart His home

And He says, "You're mine, I smiled
when I made you
I find you beautiful in every way
My love for you is fierce and
unending
I'll come to find you, whatever it
takes"

He says, "You're mine, I smiled
when I made you
I find you beautiful in every way
My love for you is fierce and
unending
I'll come to find you, whatever it
takes
My beloved"

It's time to own your belovedness

NIGHT AND DAY

Do you know about "daytime" faith and "nighttime" faith?

I recently read a book called *The Night Is Normal: A Guide through Spiritual Pain* by Alicia Britt Chole. She helped me realize that while I may be drawn to "daytime" faith (when life is going well, when connection with God comes easily, when things make sense and I can see the path before me), "nighttime" faith is just as important. We'll all walk through plenty of daylight and darkness in life, and we'll need faith in both of them. During the "night" times of faith, I can't see or hear God clearly, my questions start piling up, and I don't feel confident that things will work out. But God, in His mercy and kindness, still meets me there. It's in different ways than in the daytime, but He still meets me.

In the daytime, when people have assured me that everything will be okay, I'm able and willing to believe them. In the daytime I can receive an inspiring word from a preacher. I can operate with optimism. I feel peace because I can see God at work in my life. I can sense His closeness and hear Him speaking to me. Not so in the night. In "nighttime" faith, my spiritual senses are hindered. That's when God, whose love is steadfast, meets me in creation. I find Him in nature. In quiet silence. Until I experienced the nighttime, I didn't realize that God's language sometimes *is* silence. Mother Teresa once said, "In the silence of the heart, God speaks." Silence doesn't mean absence.

During the nighttime, trusted friends have been crucial. I've been encouraged by those who have walked through their own "dark night of the soul"—those who have come out on the other side of their own spiritual desert stronger and more in love with God than ever.

In the nighttime seasons, the Psalms have been my close companions. The Psalms represent the broad spectrum of the human experience, and the psalmists are not afraid to express their times of both joy and sorrow, complete trust and total confusion, deep faith and crippling doubt. This is what it is to be human. I'm not ashamed for struggling to believe in the dark. It's *normal.*

Our identity as God's beloved doesn't waver. It's not dependent on everything going well in our lives. It isn't based on how cheery our outlook on life is on a particular day. We are God's beloved equally in the light and in the dark.

Remember that beautiful day of my wedding I described earlier, when my husband and I were surrounded by all the people who loved us so deeply? That was a moment for daytime, shout-it-from-the-rooftops, easy-to-believe-God-loves-us kind of faith. But only a few weeks later, we were sleeping on couches in the hospital for a week because my husband's father was passing away. The commitment to love one another is not just for the good days. And you can go from the mountaintop to the valley so quickly.

Since then, my husband and I have had many beautiful, joyful moments and plenty of moments in darkness, when it was harder to discern what God was up to in our lives. But the one constant has been the sustaining, sturdy, and steadfast love of God. Therefore, we should never cease to pray, to cry out to Him. In every season, in every circumstance, the Lord hears us.

Your identity as God's Beloved is nonnegotiable. It *simply is.*

QUESTIONS TO ASK YOURSELF

When is it easiest to believe in God's steadfast love for you?

What has helped you in the moments
when faith has been a struggle?

How have you experienced God's reliable
presence with you in silence?

SCRIPTURE

SEE WHAT GREAT LOVE
THE FATHER HAS LAVISHED ON US,
THAT WE SHOULD BE CALLED
THE CHILDREN OF GOD!
AND THAT IS WHAT WE ARE!

—1 JOHN 3:1

PRAYER

God of heaven and earth, You are the One who separated the night from the day, and You have promised to be present with us in both. Thank You for the ways You show Yourself in the most joyful of days. And thank You for the ways that You show up in the dark. You are faithful through it all. Remind me that I am Your Beloved. God, I thank You that I am Yours and You are mine. Your love is steady, and it does not fail. In every moment, I am Your precious child, and You are the Father on whom I can depend.

AMEN.

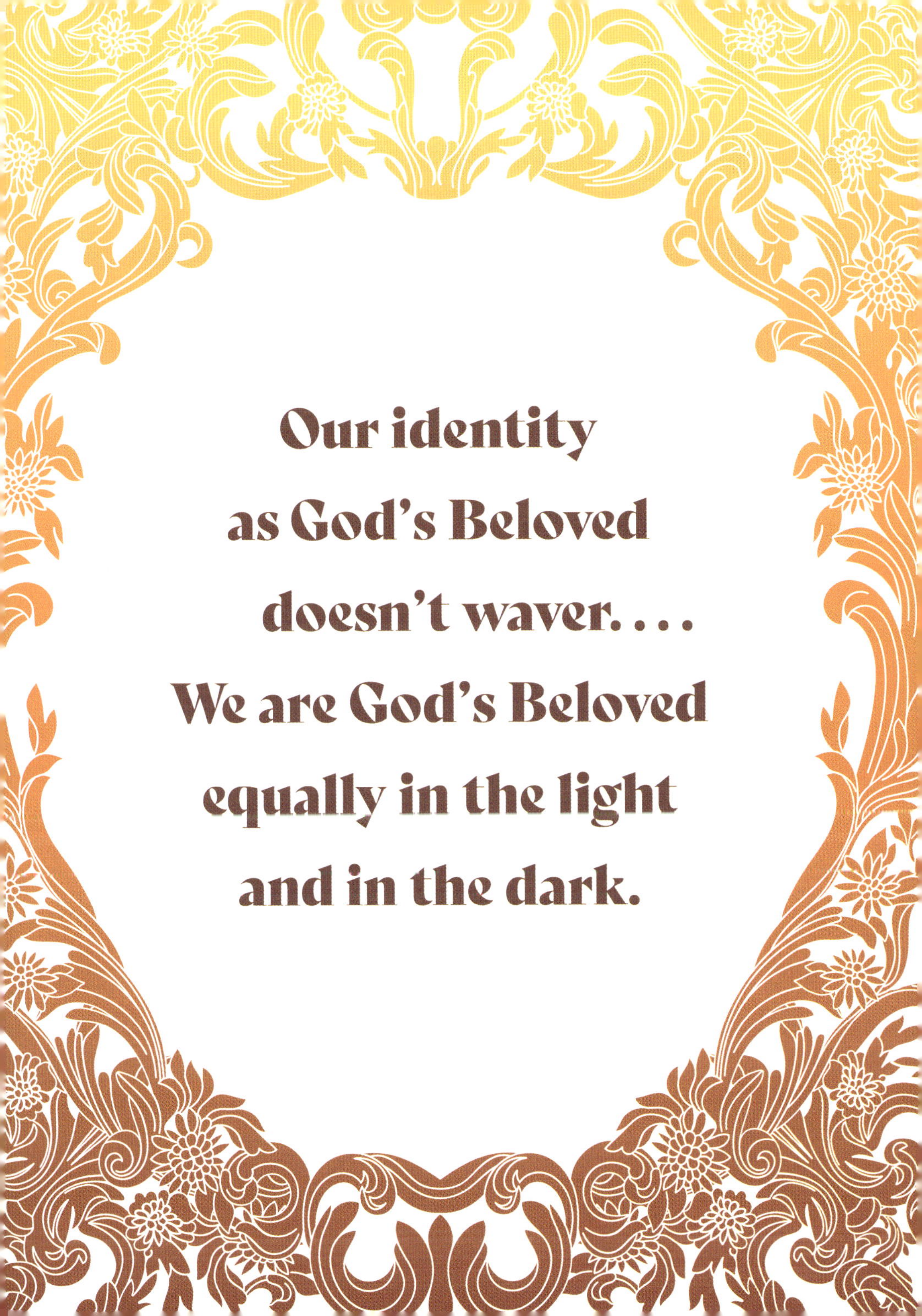
Our identity
as God's Beloved
doesn't waver. . . .
We are God's Beloved
equally in the light
and in the dark.

He says, "You're Mine, I smiled when I made you. I find you beautiful in every way. My love for you is fierce and unending. I'll come to find you, whatever it takes, My Beloved."

Belovedness

SARAH KROGER

2:36

3:42

LOVED AS YOU ARE

God loves you unconditionally, as you are and not as you should be, because nobody is as they should be."[12]

These are the words of Brennan Manning, describing his own journey with God, in *All Is Grace: A Ragamuffin Memoir*. They resonate with me because of the sneaking suspicion in my own heart that I should be something other than who and what I am. They bless me because I sometimes fear that others *tolerate* me rather than fully and unconditionally love me.

I know I'm not alone. Many people grew up in homes with parents who weren't equipped to love them the way they needed and deserved to be loved. Many people never experienced unconditional love from caregivers, or from friends, or from romantic partners. We want an everlasting love, but that type of love can't have conditions. If there are conditions, then we must "perform" in order to keep the love. And when we haven't tasted it in our human experience, it's hard to imagine that God can love us with steadfast, unconditional love.

We were designed, by God, to be *completely* loved. He does not give away His heart in small, measured, careful servings. That's

12. Brennan Manning, *All Is Grace: A Ragamuffin Memoir* (Colorado Springs: David C. Cook, 2015), 192.

why His love is often described as a tidal wave or an avalanche. You may be familiar with the story of the prodigal son. The word *prodigal* describes someone who spends what they have freely, almost recklessly. In the story, that's what the son does with his share of the inheritance. But some scholars have noted that the story could easily be called "The Prodigal Father," because that is how the father gives away his love to his children. He loves them lavishly, even when they don't deserve it. And for many of us, that complete love is so foreign to what we've known that our hearts don't always recognize it. But God does not simply tolerate you. God wants to know you and be known by you. God loves you fully and completely. God *desires* you. God smiles on you.

Near the beginning of the Bible, God gives a prayer of blessing with which the priests are to bless the Israelites:

> *The Lord bless you and keep you; the Lord make His face shine on you and be gracious to you; the Lord turn His face toward you and give you peace.* —Numbers 6:24–26

Isn't that beautiful? Can you imagine God's face shining on you? That means God is smiling. God smiled when He made you, and God delights in you when He looks at you.

If your heart is hungry to be known and embraced in this way, it's because it's what you were *made* for.

You were made to be seen, heard, and altogether known.

You were made to receive love that does not fail.

You were made to be cherished entirely and completely.

I think the work of being human is to discover this, to embrace it, and to lean into it. So many people have *no idea this is the kind of love they were made for.* That's why I want to shout it from the rooftops. I don't want anyone on this planet to *not know* that the hunger they have to be completely loved is legit. It's real. It's God-given.

I want to encourage you to spend time with the chorus of "Belovedness":

> *He says, "You're Mine, I smiled when I made you. I find you beautiful in every way. My love for you is fierce and unending. I'll come to find you, whatever it takes, My Beloved."*

Don't listen in isolation, but hear these words in conversation with all the Scriptures in these pages. Listen for God speaking to your heart. Journal what you notice. What words are easy for you to receive? Where do you notice resistance? Talk to God about why that is. Ask God to help you to receive the full truth of His unending love for you.

QUESTIONS TO ASK YOURSELF

Are you convinced that God loves you as you are and not as you should be?

Can you see the face of God *smiling* on you?

Where do you notice resistance to receiving God's love for you?

SCRIPTURE

THE LORD BLESS YOU
AND KEEP YOU;
THE LORD MAKE HIS FACE
SHINE ON YOU AND
BE GRACIOUS TO YOU;
THE LORD TURN HIS FACE
TOWARD YOU AND
GIVE YOU PEACE.

—NUMBERS 6:24–26

PRAYER

Gracious and loving Father, Your love is more than I can imagine. I struggle to wrap my mind around the perfect, unconditional love that You offer. I struggle to believe that You love me as I am. Thank You, Father. I believe that I was made to be loved completely, and I receive that love from You, right here and right now. When I look to Your face, I see Your smile. I see Your delight. In You, I am seen. In You, I am heard. In You, I am known. In You, I am loved. Today I choose to embrace the reality of Your love for me. Today I choose to own my belovedness.

AMEN.

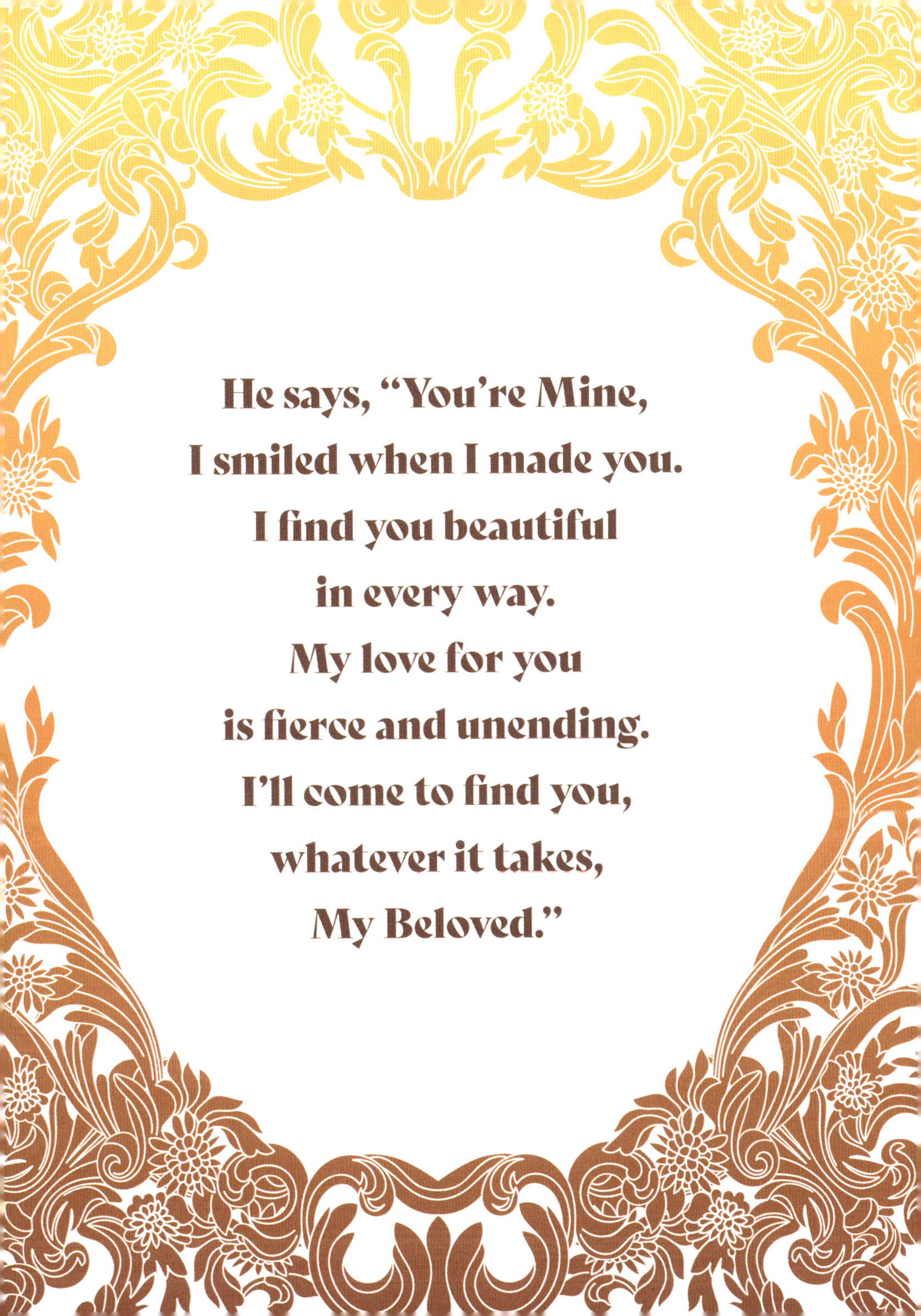
He says, "You're Mine,
I smiled when I made you.
I find you beautiful
in every way.
My love for you
is fierce and unending.
I'll come to find you,
whatever it takes,
My Beloved."

ABOUT THE AUTHOR

SARAH KROGER is a GMA Dove Award®-nominated artist, songwriter, and worship leader. With her previously released albums *Your Time* (2011), *Hallelujah Is Our Song* (2013), *Bloom* (2019), *Light* (2020), and *London Sessions* (2023), her latest project, *A New Reality*, was released May 17, 2024 (Integrity Music).

With parents involved in worship ministry, Kroger's love for music was sparked at a young age, but the impact of bullying coupled with her struggle with anxiety and shyness hid her musical talents for years. Everything changed when she met Jesus in an intimate encounter through worship at a youth conference. "Worship became my language with God," she explains. "It allowed me to communicate with the Lord in a way I hadn't experienced before...it opened my heart."

Realizing music was a gift she desired to give back to the Lord, she began leading worship around the world, drawing people from a variety of cultures and church backgrounds under the banner of Jesus. With a passion for creating a safe and prayerful space through her music, her focus has always been an authentic portrayal of her relationship with God.

With *A New Reality,* it is her hope that people will come away knowing that it's ok to question, to pull on the string and enable the unraveling to happen, knowing there is One who is gently mending the tangled threads back together into a beautiful, reconstructed tapestry.

Woven with contemplative songs that expose honest vulnerability along with corporate worship songs that express the magnificence of God, the entire collection offers new ways to see suffering, questions, and silence as building blocks for a new faith—one that is stronger because of the struggle. Sarah Kroger brings listeners into that newness by helping us all ponder the mystery of God, rest in the wonder, and see that questions are a sacred path to a new reality.

Dear Friend,

This book was prayerfully crafted with you, the reader, in mind. Every word, every sentence, every page was thoughtfully written, designed, and packaged to encourage you—right where you are this very moment. At DaySpring, our vision is to see every person experience the life-changing message of God's love. So, as we worked through rough drafts, design changes, edits, and details, we prayed for you to deeply experience His unfailing love, indescribable peace, and pure joy. It is our sincere hope that through these Truth-filled pages your heart will be blessed, knowing that God cares about you—your desires and disappointments, your challenges and dreams.

He knows. He cares. He loves you unconditionally.

BLESSINGS!
THE DAYSPRING BOOK TEAM